S0-CCE-625

ESSENTIAL PEOPLE SKILLS FOR PROJECT MANAGERS

ESSENTIAL PEOPLE SKILLS FOR PROJECT MANAGERS

Steven W. Flannes, PhD
Ginger Levin, DPA

⦀ MANAGEMENTCONCEPTS

⦅⦅⦅
MANAGEMENTCONCEPTS

8230 Leesburg Pike, Suite 800
Vienna, VA 22182
(703) 790-9595
Fax: (703) 790-1371
www.managementconcepts.com

Copyright © 2005 by Management Concepts, Inc.
All rights reserved. No part of this book may be reproduced or utilized in any form or by any means, electronic or mechanical, including photocopying, recording, or by an information storage and retrieval system, without permission in writing from the publisher, except for brief quotations in review articles.

Printed in the United States of America

Library of Congress Cataloging-in-Publication Data
Flannes, Steven, 1950–
   Essential people skills for project managers/Steven W. Flannes, Ginger Levin.
     p. cm.
   A "derivative" version based on their People skills for project managers (2001).
   Includes bibliographical references and index.
   IBSN-13: 978-1-56726-168-4 (pbk.)
   IBSN-10: 1-56726-168-X (pbk.)
   1. Project management. 2. Personnel management. 3. Emotional intelligence. 4. Social intelligence. I. Levin, Ginger. II. Flannes, Steven, 1950– People skills for project managers. III. Title.
HD69.P75F548 2005
658.3—dc22

2005045572

About the Authors

Steven W. Flannes, PhD, combines a background of leadership, management, and project leadership positions with original training as a psychologist to create a career focused on assisting individuals, teams, and organizations in improving their effectiveness in the area of the people skills required for project and career success. He has taught at the graduate level for the University of Notre Dame and the University of California, Berkeley, Extension Program. He has conducted people skills workshops for project management professionals in the United States, Canada, and the United Kingdom and is a regular presenter on regional, national, and global levels for the Project Management Institute.

Ginger Levin, DPA, is a senior consultant in project management with more than 30 years of experience. She is also an adjunct professor for the University of Wisconsin-Platteville in its Master of Science in Project Management program and serves as the university's program specialist in project management. Dr. Levin received her doctorate in public administration and information systems technology from The George Washington University (GWU), where she received the outstanding dissertation award for her research on large organizations; an MSA, with a concentration in information systems technology, also from GWU; and a BBA from Wake Forest University.

To Ann, Matt, and Jonny, who gently and warmly remind me, on a daily basis, that true excellence in the "project" of life is defined much more broadly than just through the successful achievement of the triple constraints.

—*Steve Flannes*

To my husband, Morris, for his continuing encouragement, support, and love.

—*Ginger Levin*

Table of Contents

Forewords

In the final chapter, "The Future of Project Management," of my book with Dr. Lewis R. Ireland, *Project Management: Strategic Design & Implementation* (New York: McGraw-Hill, 2002), we state that "...interpersonal skills are becoming more important." We further note that "...people skills will continue to be one of the more important assets in the management style of managers and professionals at all levels of the enterprise."

In *Essential People Skills for Project Managers*, Steven W. Flannes and Ginger Levin have expanded on these themes. They note the increasing importance of outstanding competencies in one's interpersonal skills as a prerequisite for success in the management of all types of projects. They present practical guidelines that project managers and team members can use to improve their interpersonal skills and achieve higher levels of productivity in their work.

This book offers substantial suggestions on how to handle some of the typical problems and challenges faced by team members, such as motivation, leadership styles, conflict management and resolution, and the stress that is so inherent in today's project teams. In addition, Steve and Ginger present suggestions to consider in handling critical incidents, which occur so often in project teams and require project recovery initiatives.

The concepts and processes they set forth present practical approaches that can be followed in teamwork. The authors note effective ways to handle continual challenges, such as working in a matrix management environment in a time of continual downsizing and outsourcing and in an organization where work is carried out by virtual teams in which team members may never meet face-to-face during the life of the project.

The organization of this book enables the reader to focus on areas of particular interest, with thoughtful discussion questions included at the end of each chapter. The final chapter presents a commentary on some key future issues, with an emphasis on managing one's career in project management, and suggests strategies to improve one's performance as a project manager as well as that other team members.

David I. Cleland, PhD

Why should you read this book? Quite simply, because the success of the projects you manage may depend on your understanding and application of its contents. By PMI® definition, a project is a "temporary endeavor undertaken to create a unique product, service, or result." This is a good definition that is missing only one essential piece of information: undertaken by *whom*?

As written, the definition focuses on the outcomes of a project—the products, services, or results. Much literature addresses this focus, along with the associated costs and schedules. Good project managers deliver to customers the products, services, or results that the customers paid for. But where do these come from? Do they spring mysteriously into existence through some magical process? No. They are created by *people*.

Steven W. Flannes and Ginger Levin have accomplished in this book what may be the most difficult task for any author or artist. They have looked at a final, complete work and introspectively asked themselves, "How can we make this better?" This book is more than a second edition of a previous text. It is more than a revision of content to bring it up to date with current concepts. It is a fundamental change—a book that serves project managers better in their quest for success.

Project managers are busy people. They want direct information that is useful in myriad, dynamic domains. This book succeeds on all counts. Readers will find a cut-to-the-chase approach that wastes no time with excess verbiage. They will *not* find a blunt, choppy text, but rather something that is well written and well edited to provide a cadence and flow that make reading easy—even a pleasure.

Conventional wisdom, supported by some research and anecdotal evidence, states that projects fail not on technical matters, but on "people" matters. Readers will find an expanded examination of this issue in Chapter 1, followed by a breakdown in Chapter 2 of the "people" roles that a successful project manager must play, including leader, manager, facilitator, and mentor.

Communication is the medium—the action process—through which these roles play out. It is an important and special skill that does not occur naturally in project managers or others. Chapter 3 provides comprehensive coverage of the positives to employ and the negatives to avoid.

Giving directions and obtaining results are two different actions linked by motivation. Considering individual needs is a good foundation for motivating others, but subsequent practice can devolve into a matter of rewards and punishments—the "carrot-and-stick" approach. Because projects are often implemented by matrix teams, project managers may have very little "stick." But fear only generates behavior of avoidance, not achievement. Readers will find a wealth of information in Chapter 4 on motivating in a better way.

Conflict is an omnipresent two-edged sword. It can energize and it can paralyze. The key is effective resolution. In Chapter 5, readers will learn the organizational and individual sources of conflict in project teams. They will also learn strategies and actions for resolving conflict so it does not lead to team dysfunction. Readers familiar with the "Abilene Paradox" will be reminded of—and those unfamiliar will learn—the importance of managing agreement, an aspect of project work that is as important as managing conflict.

Stress is another aspect of project life that must be faced head-on. It is a pervasive problem, arising from many sources. Eliminating stress is probably not possible, so adapting to stress becomes a critical skill. Chapter 6 describes some effective approaches and highlights others that should be avoided.

What does a project manager do when the project team or an individual team member experiences a major traumatic event? This issue is not often addressed in "people" literature. It should be, however, as it can have devastating effects on team performance. Chapter 7 provides practical approaches that readers will find helpful in these extraordinary situations.

Last, Chapter 8 offers readers an opportunity for a little reflective thinking. Having completed a journey of discovery and illumination on the "people" matters of project management, readers should take some time to consider, "What does this mean to me?" As Steve and Ginger have done, readers should examine their own past performance and ask, in light of new learning, "How can I do better?" This book provides the tools for a better tomorrow—but only for those who use them.

Kenneth H. Rose, PMP
Book Review Editor
Project Management Journal

Preface

"People issues" tend to be the most frustrating aspect of project work. People issues contribute to delays in project completion, reduced project quality, and increased project costs, not to mention high levels of personal stress and aggravation for the project management professional. Unfortunately, most project professionals, in their educational background or through other training, have had few opportunities to develop a concrete set of practical people skills.

This book is dedicated to giving you, the project management professional, tangible and field-tested people skills that will help you productively address the messy people problems that can surface on a project team, while also helping you manage your own career direction. We offer a set of specific, practical skills that you can use to resolve the difficult people issues so often encountered in managing projects.

The people skills that we present in this book include:

- The ability to communicate effectively on interpersonal levels with different types of stakeholders

- The ability to comfortably implement project manager leadership roles crucial to project success

- The ability to determine the personal style of your team members and other stakeholders, which will enable you to work more effectively with each individual

- Proven methods for productively resolving conflict

- Best practices and strategies for motivating team members

- Awareness of how to help a team recover after a critical incident has struck a team member or the team itself

- Skill and comfort in applying various approaches to managing your professional and personal stress

- Career management skills you need to thrive professionally in today's world of continual change.

Why do you need these people skills? The many reasons include the complexity of managing the people issues within a matrix management system, the increasing complexity and scope of projects, the prevailing philosophy of "doing more with less," the increasingly cross-cultural nature of teams, and the proliferation of virtual teams and an outsourced, distributed work force.

We believe this is a unique book for the project management professional. *Essential People Skills for Project Managers* is based on our original book, *People Skills for Project Managers*, published in 2001. In this derivative version, we have tried to capture the essence of the original book and bring the key concepts of people skills into sharp focus. Project managers need information they can grasp quickly and apply immediately to their projects. We hope that this "essential" version enables project managers to do just that.

We have presented parts of this book and our original *People Skills for Project Managers* to project management professionals in the United States, Canada, and the United Kingdom during two-day training workshops. We have also given presentations in Norway, Sweden, and Iceland at the International Project Management Association's NORDNET conferences, as well as to numerous chapters of the Project Management Institute in the United States. In these and similar settings, we hear from project managers just how much more attention is currently being paid—throughout the world—to the people component of project work. (Indeed, the first edition of this book was recently published in Russian by a Moscow publisher!)

We bring two different but convergent backgrounds to this book. Steve brings a background of management and leadership that builds on his original training as a clinical psychologist to a career focused on assisting individuals, teams, and organizations in working more effectively and productively. Ginger brings her background as an experienced project manager and project management consultant who has managed projects for companies and organizations in both the public and private sectors.

Two core beliefs anchored our writing. The first is that a project manager's success, advancement, and professional satisfaction are directly related to his or her level of people skills. Our second belief is that while people skills may come easier to some people than to others, everyone can significantly improve those skills by investing the time to consider the insights and practice the techniques presented in this book.

We would like to express our thanks to the staff of Management Concepts, especially Myra Strauss and Jack Knowles, for their assistance in the production of this new version.

Steven W. Flannes
Piedmont, California

Ginger Levin
Lighthouse Point, Florida

CHAPTER 1

The Importance of People Skills in Project Management

People issues in projects can be messy and uncomfortable. Most importantly for the project manager, people issues can hinder project success, especially in terms of meeting the project's schedule and budget. Achieving customer satisfaction within the project's scope and quality requirements can also be jeopardized.

As a project manager, you can, however, develop and refine tangible skills that will enable you to address people issues successfully when they surface within the project team setting. Equipped with these skills, you will not only bring added value to your organization, but you will find more personal enjoyment and fulfillment in your work as you proactively manage your career.

PROJECTS: TECHNICAL PROBLEMS WITH HUMAN DIMENSIONS

Projects are technical problems with significant human dimensions. Cleland (1999) notes that many of the skills needed for project success revolve around people skills, such as the abilities to communicate, to work with others, to negotiate, and to listen. More recently, management consultant and author Peters (2004) said that "These days, it's the people skills that matter and will increasingly determine an organization's success." From other professional perspectives comes the view that project management success is 80 percent art (the people skills) and 20 percent science- or technology-based.

Unfortunately, many project management professionals have not had training in the people skills required for success and career advancement; instead, they are forced to develop these skills informally as they proceed through their careers.

WHY ARE PEOPLE SKILLS SO IMPORTANT?

Nine reasons and trends clearly establish a current need for the project professional to have strong, specialized people skills:

- The cyclical and stage nature of projects

- The trend in organizations to become more project-based

- An increase in project complexity

- The continual downsizing and outsourcing underway in many organizations

- An increasing movement toward a customer-driven world

- The challenges of leading in a matrix management structure

- The increase of virtual teams and a distributed workplace

- The role of project managers as organizational change agents

- The use of people skills as a risk management strategy.

Cyclical and Stage Nature of Projects

The creation and nurturing of a project team involves guiding the team through the people issues encountered in all project stages.

Groups of individuals become a team by progressing through a number of distinct and sequential stages; each stage requires that the project manager and team members have finely honed people skills to succeed at the highest levels. The four project stages are:

- Coming together

- Challenge and conflict

- Doing the work

- Project and team closure.

What follows is a look at the stages through which a group of individuals becomes an effective project team. We identify the basic people skills inhererently required in each stage, and use this discussion of the four stages as a means to introduce specific people skills, each of which is covered in detail in its own chapter later in the book. Over the course of any project, all the people skills discussed in this book are actually employed simultaneously during each of the stages. Some skills are just more prominent in one stage than in another.

Coming Together Stage

A team begins as a collection of individuals with different motivations and expectations. An individual team member brings to this first stage a social schema, which is a personal belief system comprising views about how people and social systems, such as teams, should operate. People also bring stereotypes to a new system or group, which reflect that person's views and attributions toward members of various groups (e.g., "engineers," "male project managers," "older technicians about to retire").

During this stage, it is important for the project manager to resist making any assumptions about the personalities, values, sources of motivation, interests, and agendas of each of the team members.

The people skill required to refrain from making blanket assumptions about the interests and qualities of each team member is:

- The ability to perceive individual differences (personal styles and interpersonal communication styles) among team members and stakeholders (which is the subject of Chapter 3).

Working in concert with the team members during this initial project stage, the project manager must be able to articulate a vision for the project; the vision explains "why" the project is getting done (its added value), as compared to just describing the "what" of the project (the technical specifications and the deliverables).

The two people skills required for crafting and communicating the project vision are:

- Effective interpersonal communication skills (such as listening actively and asking open-ended questions, which are presented in Chapter 3)

- The project manager's ability to comfortably implement four distinct leadership roles, of which the "leadership" function is specifically used to communicate the project vision (presented in Chapter 2).

Challenge and Conflict Stage

Even in the best of teams, members often move into a second project stage that is marked by conflict and disagreement. During this stage of the project, conflict emerges because:

- Team members are attempting to clarify their roles by challenging peers for specific niches and identities

- Team members are anxious about the uncertainty involved in any new project

• Change or new experiences often contribute to the surfacing of self-doubt or old grievances.

When conflicts arise, the project manager's assertive and facilitative style helps the team create not just solutions to individual conflicts but also processes the team can use to address conflicts that resurface.

Four distinct people skills are required of the project manager to resolve initial conflict and to model positive conflict resolution behaviors:

• The ability to identify the personal styles of team members (presented in Chapter 3)

• The ability to use four interpersonal communication techniques (presented in Chapter 3)

• The ability to apply five distinct conflict resolution strategies and to know when to apply each of them (discussed in Chapter 5)

• The ability to implement the "manager" role, which is one of the four basic leadership competencies, to help the team prepare a team charter that defines the methods the team will use to resolve conflict (presented in Chapter 2).

The team charter also begins to address the project manager people skill of knowing how to address crisis situations such as when a critical incident (e.g., serious illness, death of a team member, natural disaster) strikes a team member or the team itself.

The project manager people skill of knowing how to respond effectively to a critical incident involves the abilities (discussed in Chapter 7) to:

• Assess whether a critical incident debriefing (i.e., a facilitated team meeting designed to talk through the crisis) is warranted for the team

- Be empathic to the team members' personal reactions to the event while still maintaining a business-oriented, task-completion focus

- Know when a project recovery plan is needed, plus the ability to identify the qualities of the ideal project recovery manager.

However, one of the potential negative aspects of creating standards and group norms via a team charter is that the team may begin to display conformity, obedience, or "group think" in decision making. Group think is defined as team behavior that displays extreme cooperation, compliance, and little willingness to appropriately confront the ideas of other team members. This risk arises when team members are conflict-averse, when the project manager is very directive, and when team size increases.

To mitigate the risk of group think and conformity, the project manager needs to achieve a balance of cohesion and dissent; this process is also known as "managing agreement" on the project team. The people skills required for managing agreement involve five conflict resolution skills (presented in Chapter 5). As the team begins to address this stage of conflict by using these skills, the team starts to evolve into the next stage, which involves getting the bulk of the work done.

Doing the Work Stage

When handled smoothly, the process of creating team standards for dealing with issues such as conflict resolution allows the group to do what it has been charged to do: complete the project within the guidelines of specifications, time, and cost.

To keep the team moving forward in a positive and productive manner, the project manager needs to create the conditions for:

- An adequately resourced team

- A proactively motivated team.

The two people skills required of the project manager to obtain the needed resources for the team and to create a motivated team atmosphere are:

- Comfort implementing the leadership role of "facilitator," which involves an assertive pursuit of needed resources (discussed in Chapter 2)

- The ability to employ a variety of motivational approaches tailored to each individual on the team (covered in Chapter 4).

Should the project manager find that the team is not operating with the expected level of efficiency during this stage, certain people issues may be getting in the way. It is important at this point for the project manager to conduct a "people-issues audit" to determine if these issues are causing the project to veer off track.

Conducting a "people issues" audit involves:

- Determining if the team has an accurate grasp of the project vision, which encompasses a description of the added value the project brings to the customer (Chapter 2)

- Using people skills for managing conflict (Chapter 5) and motivating team members (Chapter 4)

- Fulfilling the project leadership role of "facilitator" (Chapter 2) by spending enough time developing needed support and resources for the project with important stakeholders both internal and external to the organization.

Project and Team Closure Stage
From the people-issue perspective of project management, the last stage is the one in which individuals on the team, and the team as a whole, assess the level of goal achievement and begin the process of "saying good-bye."

This closure process affects team members differently, and their reactions are often directed toward the project manager. During this period, the manager is trying hard to conclude the remaining pieces of the project and may be surprised at the range of feelings team members display.

When facing project closure, the people-oriented project manager should remember that:

- Team members may display a wide range of unforeseen feelings, such as anger, apprehension, fear, and lack of confidence.

- These feelings may not be logical and can have very little to do with events or issues related to the project team.

This is also the stage in which the team members begin to think about what they will be doing after this project is completed. This future orientation is natural, given the self-protective need to manage one's career in project work.

Two distinct people skills are required of the project manager to address these team member career concerns:

- The "mentor" role (discussed in Chapter 2), in which the project manager, in conjunction with the functional manager, gently guides the team member toward a frank discussion of the next assignment

- The application of six specific, active career management skills (which are examined in Chapter 8).

In this last phase of the project, stakeholders also may be experiencing personal stress (in the form of anxiety, lowered mood, and irritation) as well as physical fatigue. Under these conditions, the project manager must work to keep the team members committed to completing the tasks in a way that does not allow that stress to hamper performance.

To maximize performance at the close of the project, the project manager needs to use the people skills of:

- Crafting tailored motivation strategies that address the individual differences of team members (described in Chapter 4)

- Offering suggestions or modeling five specific stress management techniques that can help keep team member performance at optimal levels (described in Chapter 6).

Various skills are required to address the people issues that arise during each of the stages of a typical project. While the successful project manager uses almost all of these people skills during each stage, throughout the book we have tried to highlight the most important skills needed during each stage.

Trend in Organizations to Become More Project-Based

Organizations are becoming more and more project-based. Flat, flexible organizational structures are becoming the norm, replacing the hierarchical, bureaucratic structures of the past. As organizations become flatter, the project manager's interactions with internal and external stakeholders increases, calling for an enhanced ability to apply people skills to a greater variety of people and personalities.

This trend toward the projectization of the workplace is evidenced by the number of people who identify themselves as project professionals. When our first edition of *People Skills for Project Managers* was published in 2001, the Project Management Institute (PMI®) had approximately 77,000 members. As we write this edition in early 2005, PMI® reports that membership has increased to over 150,000 members in more than 150 countries. Clearly, such a steep rise in membership suggests that the project model of working is taking off on a global scale within organizations and companies, and that project management is the career choice of many professionals.

As organizations have become more project-based, a shift in management style has occurred—a shift requiring effective people skills. This management style, exemplified by the influenced-based project manager, is consensual and participative, calling for the project manager to serve as facilitator, team member, team player, and coach; hence, the importance of being able to demonstrate exceptional people skills has increased.

Verma (1997) presents some additional reasons for the need to change to a new method of management that has implications for people skills. Verma explains that rapidly changing technology and an increasingly competitive society have made the need to share information throughout the organization a critical success factor. With this need to share information comes the requirement that the project manager be skilled in communicating on both the individual and group levels—and able to communicate effectively with different styles of personalities in different cultures.

Increase in Project Complexity

The trend toward increasingly complex projects also creates a need for people skills. The norm today in project work is to work faster, with fewer resources, turning out products and services with multiple end applications and uses.

The complexity of projects is also seen through the window of continually advancing technological developments. The role of the project manager becomes more complex as he or she struggles to maintain an adequate level of technological knowledge while still responding to the human factors of the team in an atmosphere of intense competition from other organizations. With the expansion of virtual teams, project complexity has also increased as global teams are now capable of working on a project around the clock.

Continual Downsizing and Outsourcing

Not long ago, downsizing and outsourcing in organizations were exceptions rather than the norm and occurred only in times of economic slowdown. People joined an organization and tended to remain with it for their entire careers, many in the same functional area or field.

Downsizing and outsourcing have become a way of life for many organizations. Frame (1994) explains that downsizing is one way that companies can become "lean and mean." Organizations have limited resources, and they need to expend those resources in productive areas.

Ironically, companies experiencing rapid growth in one sector may elect to downsize in other departments or units or to out-source these functions completely. For example, it is common to see a newspaper article announcing layoffs in an organization, and in the same paper or on a website, to see advertisements for job openings in the same company.

With downsizing and outsourcing now the norm within most organizations, project managers face people issues such as:

- Finding ways to motivate the "surviving" employees, who may be wondering if their jobs will be the next to go

- Motivating these same employees, who now operate under the mandate of "doing more with less."

Movement Toward Customer-Driven Projects

Today, projects are customer-driven, as both internal and external customers assume an active role in the project from beginning to end. Customer understanding and support can no longer be taken for granted. Building and maintaining relationships with customers is a continual process for the project leader and team. It is no longer safe to assume that a relationship will continue simply because the organization has worked with a customer for a long time.

In addition to delivering a quality technical product or service, today's project manager must also have the people skills that contribute to customer relationship management and customer retention. Project professionals are now measured by how well they interact with their customers and how well they work to enhance existing business opportunities with current customers. Business development, by necessity, is a major aspect of everyone's job. Customer involvement, however, must be nurtured. A key goal is to understand the customer, which involves the people skills of good interpersonal techniques.

Leading in a Matrix Management Structure

The matrix organization has emerged as the organizational structure of choice for projects. Roles and responsibilities are uncertain in the matrix structure, and the successful project manager needs a variety of people skills to succeed in such an environment.

The matrix structure tends to discourage team member commitment to a project. Each team member understands that his or her assignment to a project is temporary. Team members may never again work with the project manager and the other team members once the project ends. They may also be supporting multiple projects and working for several project managers simultaneously, further diffusing their commitment to a single project or project manager. Within this mix of conflicting loyalties and commitments, the project manager must be able to apply people skills to motivate each team member.

Kerzner (1998) highlights the motivational issues facing the project manager in a matrix system when he notes that:

- Project managers have little real authority; functional managers have considerable authority

- Project managers may not have input into team members' performance evaluations; functional managers are responsible for employee evaluations.

Increase of Virtual Teams and a Distributed Workplace

The virtual organization has emerged to meet the challenges of unprecedented growth, customer expectations and alternatives, global competition, complexity, rapid change, and time-to-market compression. Customers, suppliers, and employees no longer reside in the same city, but in different time zones and on different continents. The virtual organization may quickly deploy its resources to form project teams capable of responding to emerging project work. As Rad and Levin state (2003), managing organizations by projects has become the norm with the use of virtual teams because projects are no longer limited by physical boundaries. The virtual organization is the model for the future.

Such an environment presents many people-oriented challenges. It is harder to develop a group identity, share information, recognize team member strengths and weaknesses, and develop trust. Haywood (1998) investigated project managers' perceptions of the management of virtual project teams compared with traditional, co-located teams. She found that project managers clearly perceive more difficulty in managing virtual teams, particularly in the area of communication; hence the need for exceptional communication skills for the virtual team manager. Rad and Levin (2003) further note that because the virtual team may span multiple cultural and language boundaries, the project's procedures must provide guidelines that ensure that the resulting diversity is an asset and not a liability.

The virtual project manager must have people skills that allow him or her to:

- Be a leader (using influence) rather than a controller or supervisor

- Create trust and an identity among the virtual team members, allowing them to feel free to discuss ideas without being dismissed arbitrarily.

Role of Project Managers as Change Agents

Organizations must make changes in the face of global competition and technological obsolescence. In light of the trend toward management by projects, in addition to the obvious role of completing quality projects, the project manager must now also be a change agent.

Change within organizations causes tension, which may result in lower morale, higher anxiety, more stress, and reduced productivity. In altering the organizational culture to make it more project-based, the project manager will often experience resistance, perhaps even from the most senior levels of management, who may view the project model as a threat to the power they believe they hold within the current functional model. Many project managers have commented on the chief executive officer (CEO) who says that the company should move toward working as a project-based organization, only to find that same CEO putting up various forms of resistance to implementing this change.

The project manager acting as a change agent must be able to demonstrate the people skills of:

- Articulating the vision to stakeholders at different organizational levels

- Being assertive and persistent in pursuing the organizational transformation

- Applying good listening skills.

Use of People Skills for Risk Management

All projects encounter risks of some type. The sheer size and complexity of today's projects places increased emphasis on managing risks. While risk management usually focuses on the deliverables of the project, it must also focus on the people component of the project; after all, projects are performed by people.

The effective project manager needs good people skills to manage the people risks in an organization. Managing these risks involves people skills in relationship management, which can reduce:

- Grievances, harassment complaints, and Equal Employment Opportunity Commission complaints

- Union activity

- Violence in the workplace

- Loss of key staff members and other retention issues

- Time lost to injuries.

In commenting on the people components of risk management, Frame (1999) suggests that if one compiled a list of risks for a project, the list of possible human risks would be the longest. He also believes that it is difficult to determine appropriate risk management responses in advance, creating a need for spontaneous, people skills-based solutions rather than the implementation of predefined contingency plans.

WHAT CAN A PROJECT MANAGER DO TO IMPROVE KEY PEOPLE SKILLS?

To help a project manager achieve project and career success, the subsequent chapters of this book offer:

- Approaches to follow in project leadership

- Methods to use for identifying individual differences among team members

- Techniques for interpersonal communications

- Best practices to follow to motivate team members

- Methods for resolving conflicts productively

- Ways to respond effectively when a critical incident strikes a project team

- Techniques for managing personal stress

- Skills required for proactive career management.

Chapter 2 discusses the four different roles a project manager must assume: leader, manager, facilitator, and mentor.

Chapter 3 addresses the importance of developing tangible interpersonal communication skills and provides a model for identifying different types of team members with differing personality styles.

Chapter 4 delves into the art of how to motivate individual team members as well as the team as a unit. Common motivation mistakes and pitfalls are addressed to guide the project manager in reducing the risks involved in implementing these approaches.

Chapter 5 describes the inherent benefits and disadvantages of conflict and presents five specific approaches for addressing conflict. Insights are offered into preferred personal styles of managing conflict, along with the benefits and limitations of these styles.

Chapter 6 challenges the project manager to create a personal stress management plan for addressing the pressures of leading today's complex projects. Specific, research-based stress management techniques are described.

Chapter 7 covers the steps that a project manager should take when a tragedy (a "critical incident") such as the unexpected death of a team member strikes the project team. Tangible resources that a project manager can offer the team during these difficult periods are presented, with the goal of helping team members return to pre-crisis levels of performance.

Chapter 8 concludes the book with thoughts about developing an ongoing personal performance plan, suggesting concrete career management "people skills" that every project manager should have and providing a model to use in exploring the human component of project work.

Our purpose in writing *Essential People Skills for Project Managers* is to provide tools, techniques, and perspectives on the many people challenges of the project management profession. Use these tools to help you solve some problems, increase your value to your organization, experience the many positive aspects of managing project teams, and work closely with your team members—in essence, to enrich your work leading project teams. This is an exciting time to be a project manager!

CHAPTER 2

Project Manager: Leader, Manager, Facilitator, Mentor

Project managers, like many other leaders, are often promoted into leadership roles for reasons related to technical competency rather than because they have demonstrated leadership and management skills.

Ideally, project managers gradually acquire essential leadership skills during their early years of project work. They may also develop and sharpen their leadership skills by working with seasoned mentors or by attending formal project leadership training offered by professional organizations and institutes.

Regardless of the developmental method, the project manager must acquire a solid knowledge of basic leadership and management skills. These skills in leading team members are crucial because, ultimately, the success or failure of all projects is founded on the "people" component.

In many ways, a project manager faces greater leadership challenges than a functional manager does. In essence, the project manager must be able to implement four distinct roles or leadership functions over the life of a project—and must master the people skills that are needed to fulfill these leadership functions.

The four key roles of the project manager are:

- Leader

- Manager

- Facilitator

- Mentor.

PROJECT MANAGER VERSUS FUNCTIONAL MANAGER

The project manager faces a more complex set of leadership challenges than the functional manager does, and therefore is required to have a more sophisticated set of people skills that can be applied to meet those leadership challenges. Some of the distinct leadership challenges between the project manager and the functional manager revolve around:

- Clarity of organizational structure

- Consistency of human resources

- Sources of leverage for motivation.

Clarity of Organizational Structure

The relationship between the functional manager and the employee is ongoing, which provides the functional manager greater clarity of organizational structure. This ongoing nature provides stability as team members develop deeper working relationships with peers and the manager. The ongoing nature of the functional unit also provides clarity of mission, as the purpose of the unit's functioning (i.e., its product or service) generally remains constant over time. Such constancy offers opportunities for organizational efficiencies because formal and informal operating methods tend to remain constant.

Consistency of operation also exists for the functional manager based on his or her ability to control individuals in terms of assigning work tasks and providing direction. In addition, the leadership focus is clearer for the functional manager because he or she has fewer stakeholders and customers. The functional manager is also able to focus more clearly on managing upward, as the result of a clear and ongoing reporting relationship with his or her superior.

The project manager, in contrast, faces much less clarity of organizational structure. By definition, the project team, whether co-located or virtual, comes together for a finite time and mission and is required to achieve deliverables within aggressive time frames. The organizational structure is often nebulous, as team members come and go. The project manager has no direct authority to control all the activities of team members since many of them work on numerous projects simultaneously.

In the context of this lack of organizational clarity, as well as the lack of designated authority to control the work of the team members, the project manager needs a specific set of people skills to succeed. The sophisticated people skills required of the project manager in a matrix model include:

- A high tolerance for ambiguity

- Personal comfort in operating with a dual focus (such as applying technical skills while also operating as a generalist)

- The ability to quickly envision how the organizational functioning of each new team should come together

- A tolerance for relinquishing control while maintaining an achievement motivation

- Skill in creating group cohesion without succumbing to "group think" (see Chapter 5 for tips on avoiding group think on a team)

- A personal level of confidence that allows him or her to undertake a significant endeavor (the new project) without knowing potential obstacles.

It is often difficult for the project manager to identify methods for developing people skills. Skills such as tolerance for ambiguity, strong self-confidence, and comfort with relinquishing control are often best developed through:

- Becoming involved in mentoring relationships

- Choosing assignments outside of your comfort zone

- Seeking honest feedback from peers/mentors who know your work

- Taking classes and experiential workshops outside of your comfort zone.

Consistency of Human Resources

The functional manager also experiences greater consistency than the project manager does in the area of human resources.

Because of the long-term nature of the working relationships in the functional unit, the functional manager has more exposure to the technical strengths and weaknesses of each employee, as well as information about each employee's personality and idiosyncrasies. Such knowledge allows the functional manager to:

- Apply the human resource strengths of the unit more effectively

- Avoid problems by slotting people into tasks in which they are likely to succeed.

Because the working relationships in the functional unit are long-term in nature, the functional manager also has the advantage, from the perspective of developing the human resources of the unit, to:

- Create and monitor ongoing personal development plans for each employee, thus increasing the level of the unit's talent pool

- Be involved in hiring individuals for the unit.

The project manager, however, faces a much tougher set of challenges regarding the human resources capability on his or her team. Challenges include:

- Trying to quickly assess the strengths and weaknesses of people with whom he or she has never previously worked

- Having little control over the human resources component of the team, as team members are often assigned to the team by someone else

- Having little time or authority to craft long-term professional development plans for the poorly performing team member; often, the project manager has to take what is given and make the most of it.

The project manager needs specific people skills to be able work effectively within these human resource constraints. These people skills include:

- The ability to quickly and accurately assess the strengths, weaknesses, and personalities of people he or she may never have met (see Chapter 3 for more on this ability to identify individual differences)

- The ability to focus more on the strengths of the team member (seeing the glass half full) as compared to ruminating over what the team member cannot do and wishing that someone "better" had been assigned to the project.

These two skills are best developed by:

- Developing knowledge of and comfort with a system that describes individual differences (see Chapter 3 for a discussion of the Myers-Briggs Type Indicator)

- Monitoring your own tendency to see the glass as either half full or half empty, and consciously working on identifying some positive aspects of any negative professional situation (see Chapter 6 for a discussion of positive psychology).

Sources of Leverage for Motivation

The functional manager faces a less complex challenge in the area of motivation than the project manager does.

Because the relationships within a functional unit are long-term, the employee realizes that he or she will need to meet the expectations of the manager, who will have significant impact on raises, promotions, assignments, and career direction. Within this ongoing relationship, the employee generally carries an intrinsic motivation to please the functional manager and to work through any difficulties in the working relationship. In essence, these sanctioned powers give the functional manager the ability to motivate with the "stick" as compared to the "carrot." (See Chapter 4 describes for more appropriate tools to use than the "stick.")

For the project manager, the process of motivating the team is far more difficult. In a matrix organization, the project manager has little control over team member availability and therefore must lead the team more through influence and motivation than through direction. The project manager must be truly skilled in influencing the behavior of team members, creatively using many "carrots."

To motivate team members effectively through influence, the project manager needs two key people skills:

- The ability to motivate individuals through knowledge of their personal styles and career stages

- The ability to apply sophisticated interpersonal communication skills.

These two people skills required for successfully motivating team members in a matrix organizational structure are described in detail in Chapters 3 and 4.

THE FOUR LEADERSHIP ROLES OF THE PROJECT MANAGER

With so much information available on leadership, it is difficult to pick one model or theory that adequately describes the key skills and attributes necessary for successful project management leadership.

Our model of project manager leadership involves a melding of the many disparate theories of leadership into four distinct leadership roles that a project manager will play at different points along the evolution of a project. These four complementary roles involve the project manager as a leader, manager, facilitator, and mentor (see Table 2-1).

Table 2-1. Roles of the Project Manager

Role	Key Behaviors
Leader	Conceptualize and articulate the project vision. Motivate team members toward the vision. Represent the team to stakeholders.
Manager	Create a project administrative structure. Track compliance with performance, cost, and time. Report status to stakeholders.
Facilitator	Communicate clearly, both verbally and in writing. Model and create methods for resolving conflict. Empower team members to act with volition and confidence. Proactively obtain needed project resources.
Mentor	Model appropriate team, professional, and organizational behaviors. Help team members identify possibilities for problem-solving and career path development. Display genuine personal interest in team members' performance and development.

These four roles should not viewed as distinct categories of behavior. Rather, they represent four key functions that a project manager is simultaneously discharging at any point during the work day. Even during the same conversation with a team member, a project manager may seamlessly move from one of the four functions to another.

Generally, each project manager has a preference or comfort in adopting one or two of the four roles. As you consider these roles, notice which is most comfortable for you. Then develop a plan to develop the people skills and comfort level required to perform the other roles.

Project Manager as "Leader"

The leadership role involves the projects manager's ability to define the vision for the project, and then to sell that vision to the team members and other stakeholders. The vision is the "why" of the project; it articulates the mission of the effort and the added value it brings to the organization and the customer. The vision also demonstrates how the team's end product or service fits into the larger scale of the company's efforts—the big picture of why effort and resources are being expended.

In crafting a vision for the project, the project manager integrates the perspectives and goals of the customer as well as the perspectives of the team members and other stakeholders. Without actively talking with the customer about the true purpose and creating this personal representation, the project manager may begin the project with only a partial understanding of the scope and deliverables. This can lead to potential problems in terms of scope creep and extensive changes to accommodate the customer's requirements.

The project manager must then create a personal representation of the true purpose of the project, noting subtle goals and the customer's definition of added value. If the project manager feels confident that he or she knows the customer's true needs, the resulting representation will enable the project to begin with motivation and purpose.

When operating in this leadership role of crafting the project vision, the project manager needs to demonstrate the following people skills:

- Ask probing questions that demonstrate an interest in taking initial discussions beyond the general level

- Recognize what the customer is saying and not saying, which can be equally important in defining project objectives and requirements

- Clarify perceptions of the project's purpose, ensuring that the both the project manager and the customer are working in the same direction.

The next step in the role of leader is for the project manager to begin a dialogue with the team members regarding the project's purpose. This discussion is not a one-time event to be completed at the project kickoff meeting, nor is it a one-way discussion in which the leader presents the purpose to the group in a formal briefing. Instead, it is highly interactive and ongoing. The project manager strives to encourage team members to define the vision in their own words, believing that a personal definition of project mission:

- Has more meaning for individual team members

- Allows them to become more engaged in the process.

The leader role is also demonstrated at the beginning of the project when the project manager endeavors to establish personal credibility with the team members. Establishing credibility or "walking the talk" involves demonstrating actions and behaviors that are consistent with verbally espoused values.

When a leader's actions are consistent with his or her spoken values, the leader's behavior is said to be congruent. Leader congruence is crucial for creating a motivating climate for the team (see Chapter 6 for more on congruent behavior).

The people skills required for leader "congruence" include the ability to:

- Identify behaviors that you can reasonably expect to demonstrate as being consistent with your values

- Refrain from over-promising to deliver on something that may not be possible because of organizational resource limitations or political constraints

- Seek feedback from a mentor, coach, or supportive colleague regarding how congruent your behavior is with your stated values.

Leadership for the project manager also involves an active role as the team's voice to the outside world. The leader needs to communicate actively with both internal and external stakeholders:

- Supporting and obtaining buy-in to project goals

- Providing updates and progress reports

- Addressing conflict situations in a productive and forthright manner.

In summary, the leader role for the project manager involves answering the question "Why are we doing this project?" by painting a picture of the mission and the added value the completed project will represent.

Project Manager as "Manager"

The manager role, viewed from the perspective of people challenges, involves creating an administrative system with enough structure and discipline to get the job done without having that structure stretch into the realm of excessive bureaucracy.

The creation of this type of administrative system is often easier said than done, with the balance between structure and team member freedom of functioning varying from project to project depending on the mix of the individuals on the team.

The manager function involves creating an infrastructure that allows team members to thrive during periods of uncertainty.

A project is similar to life: We hope we know what is going to happen, but the reality is that we are continually surprised, often in ways that place significant demands on us. Such project unpredictability is reduced if the project leader has created team operating structures that are clear, reasonable, efficient, and not overly bureaucratic.

Examples of team structures where the project manager has successfully fulfilled the role of manager include situations where:

- Team member roles and responsibilities provide a clear source of direction, while still giving each team member opportunities to define his or her own path to complete them. This can be done by using a resource assignment matrix tied to the project's work breakdown structure that shows specific responsibilities for each team member (e.g., approve, coordinate, review, perform).

- Processes and procedures state clear behavioral and performance expectations as guidelines rather than as strict rules that must be followed without exception.

- Meetings are purposeful and focused, providing opportunities to balance the need to dissent and discuss with the need to decide and seek closure.

The project manager who successfully meets the goals of the manager function discusses these structure-setting requirements with the team, explaining the rationale for what some team members may perceive as excessive structure. In those discussions, it is helpful for the project manager operating as a manager to:

- Talk about what flexibility may be possible

- Consider the individual needs of each team member

- State the preference to complete the project with a minimum of bureaucratic structure.

Personal issues and style will also affect the manner in which the project manager discharges the manager role. Some project managers will have a tendency to create excessive structure (i.e., become too controlling), while others will have a tendency to create too little structure (i.e., adopt a more laissez-faire approach to managing). Both approaches are problematic.

The overcontrolling manager has difficulty prioritizing how best to spend his or her time and often focuses on tasks that may be better handled by others. Although well-intentioned, this project manager strives for excessive structure and order, perhaps reflecting underlying doubt that things will work out. Undercurrents of anxiety and personal worry are common for this type of leader, who is frequently unaware of how his or her behavior affects the attitude and morale of project team members.

Team members working with a micromanaging manager react with feelings such as:

- Frustration, anger, and irritation about being over-structured or over-managed

- Loss of motivation for completing project tasks

- Perception of being undervalued or unappreciated.

If the project manager believes that such behaviors are a risk, then he or she should seek regular feedback from the team regarding perceptions of over-structure and over-control. Ask direct questions since team members tend not to volunteer this type of information.

The laissez-faire manager, conversely, tends to put too little structure in place for the project team, allowing many details or processes to drift. This person may be too trusting of team members to follow through and, as a result, may tend to overlook matters such as compliance with the project management methodology or the timely completion of tasks.

In many cases, a laissez-faire manager is more enamored with creating a vision for the project, as compared with implementing the vision on a tactical level. If a manager errs on the side of creating too little structure for the team, the risks are that:

- Project tasks, compliance, and monitoring and may suffer

- Team members may appear anxious and hesitant about how to proceed, believing that they do not have enough specifics or systems to be successful.

Clearly, the "right" place to be on this continuum is in the middle, where a structure is in place but team members still possess autonomy and flexibility to follow their own paths.

Defining an idealized point on the continuum of over-controlling structure versus laissez-faire is difficult, but indicators of an appropriate balance between these extremes include signs such as:

- Team members report that sufficient procedures are in place for the team to operate in an autonomous manner

- Key work can be tracked and monitored in a setting where team members demonstrate positive attitudes, initiative, and creativity

- Basic reports to stakeholders are prepared without team members complaining about meaningless requirements.

Project Manager as "Facilitator"

Facilitation is one of the most subtle, yet profound roles the project manager can assume. Project facilitation involves the project manager demonstrating behaviors and attitudes that help others get their work done.

Facilitation is often achieved through the art of influencing others. It involves communicating effectively, resolving conflicts, obtaining needed resources, and motivating people, both individually and as a team.

People skills required for the facilitator role include:

• Using clear statements that get to the point

• Asking open-ended questions, such as "What else do you think our team needs to be successful on this project?"

• Being a good listener by trying to recognize the key points of the speaker's message

• Clarifying the meaning of the speaker's message by asking if your understanding is correct

• Demonstrating willingness to use assertive behaviors to get the resources your team needs, coupled with a tolerance for not being liked by outside stakeholders.

Facilitation as a management skill can be compared with the role of planning and orchestrating the details for a dinner party.

The host of the party does his or her best to consider the needs of the guests, to obtain the items needed for the event, and to create an atmosphere appropriate for the gathering. As the guests arrive, the host continues facilitating the event by offering choices to the guests and doing what he or she can to create a positive experience.

However, this is where "facilitation" ends. The host cannot make the people have a good time. Facilitation provides them with the resources they need, but the creation of the "fun" part is up to the individuals involved.

The goal in facilitation is to provide team members with choices, options, and a conducive setting, and then trust that the team will create the sought-after outcome. In this role, it is not the project manager's job to create the solution on his or her own—that is up to the team.

A project manager who is adept at helping team members address and resolve conflict in a productive manner is also demonstrating facilitation skills. So is the manager who anticipates resource needs and proactively obtains needed supplies, materials, technology, and human resources.

As a leadership role, facilitation requires that the project manager not get too involved in the details or substance of the project. Such immersion in the details, while intellectually stimulating for the project manager, can become a way to avoid some of the less pleasant aspects of being the facilitator—such as the need to use assertive behavior to make things happen for the team.

As a people skill, the assertiveness component of the facilitator role can be developed by reading books and attending workshops on assertive behavior.

Project Manager as "Mentor"

Mentoring is the process by which one person (the mentor) assists another person (the mentee), either formally or informally, in various tasks related to professional growth and development.

The mentor role for the project manager is a valuable contribution to team member performance and development, but it is a service that needs to be offered with the utmost care. Some team members do not want to be in a mentoring relationship with their current project manager; they may prefer to receive their mentoring from their functional manager or from another senior project manager located in another part of the organization. Nonetheless, the project manager can accomplish some of the development aspects of mentoring a current team member by offering the mentoring input in a casual and indirect manner that aids the team member's growth while also addressing current work issues on the project.

> Mentoring actions and behaviors may include any of the following people skills, depending on the needs of the individual team member and the current needs of the project:
>
> - Serving as a role model, by which the project leader demonstrates skills, behaviors, and attitudes whose adoption may benefit team members
>
> - Demonstrating a genuine, personal interest in the welfare and professional growth of team members
>
> - Offering suggestions, possibilities, resources, problem-solving approaches, and opportunities to think out loud with team members regarding current or future issues
>
> - Providing feedback that is supportive yet frank and accurate, reinforcing successes while portraying failures as learning opportunities
>
> - Offering motivation directed toward assisting team members in identifying and achieving long-term professional goals.

During the more intense periods of a project, most interactions between the project manager and a team member are focused on real-time issues. A mentoring emphasis during those periods is not appropriate and should wait until work demands have lessened. These quieter times are when the project manager in the mentor role and the team member can debrief each other about recent work; the mentor can then offer formal or informal guidance about how the team member could approach such a situation in the future.

Sometimes a team member will request such feedback from the project manager; other times, he or she will not request this type of feedback but will be receptive if it is offered. Clearly, the project manager needs to develop a knowledge of the personalities of the team members with an eye toward identifying those individuals who might be receptive to mentoring.

In many organizations, a mentoring relationship is best suited to a more formal relationship between a project manager and a person on another project team. Such a relationship often enables both parties to focus more clearly on the developmental needs of the mentee, free of distractions that can arise when both parties are working on the same team.

Mentees often describe the mentoring relationship as a positive one where they can talk in confidence with a professional outside of their project team on matters of professional growth and development. Mentors report positive feelings about the opportunity to give something back to the profession in terms of assisting a junior colleague in moving along the career path.

The leadership challenges for the project manager are more complicated than the challenges facing the functional leader. The project manager faces greater leaderships hurdles in the areas of clarity of organizational structure, consistency of human resources, and motivation of team members.

The leadership roles of the project manager are multifaceted. The project manager must simultaneously serve as leader, manager, facilitator, and mentor.

The leadership role requires that the project manager provide a vision to the team that defines the added value the project will bring to the customer. The manager role helps provide a structure to keep the focus on the customer in terms of performance, time, and cost. The facilitator role involves providing the necessary emotional and logistical support that team members need to complete the project. Finally, the mentor role asks the project manager to artfully assist team members with issues of professional growth, development, and direction.

It is rare that a project manager excels equally in all four of these leadership roles. The project manager needs to be realistic about strengths and weaknesses in the four leadership roles (without being self-critical) and should actively pursue professional development for those aspects of leading, managing, facilitating, or mentoring that need improvement. It is also important that the project manager develop the ability to recognize when a specific role is appropriate and how and when to move from one role to another.

Discussion Questions

A project manager working for an aerospace company near San Diego is placed in charge of a project whose team members are junior-level professionals with little experience working on their own. This presents a problem for the project manager, because the bulk of the work on the project is to be conducted by a virtual team, with most of the team members scattered across the country.

This project manager has managed teams before, but these teams were staffed with senior professionals, each with a history of self-directed performance and all working at the same geographical location. She makes the false assumption that this group can be managed in a laissez-faire style, with her leaving much of the direction up to the team.

As the project evolves, problems surface because the laissez-faire style is not working. This group of junior staff members requires more monitoring and structure than the project manager assumed they would need. This problem stems from their junior status, the virtual nature of the team, and the project encountering production problems that could have been avoided with tighter monitoring by the project manager.

1. How can this project manager now establish a more structured managerial approach?

2. How can this project manager best mentor some of the junior-level team members?

3. How can this project manager ensure that all the team members share the same concept of the project's objectives and scope?

CHAPTER 3

Interpersonal Communication Tools for the Project Manager

The project manager has a variety of tools for use in the workplace. These tools include information technology, project management methodologies, engineering expertise, estimating, earned value, financial forecasting, and budget management.

One tool that is rarely considered in detail is the tool of interpersonal communication. The project manager can make effective use of this tool to increase the team's performance.

Key interpersonal communication skills include the abilities to:

- Develop concrete communication skills, which can serve as "the nuts and bolts" of an effective discussion

- Identify and appreciate individual differences among stakeholders

- Pay attention to the tone and texture of the communication

- Recognize communication "stoppers."

DEVELOPING CONCRETE COMMUNICATION SKILLS

Several basic communication skills and techniques are crucial for effective communication. These are skills that can be practiced and improved, and even small improvements in fine tuning these skills will pay big dividends.

Sending "I" Messages

Sending "I" messages, such as "I believe there is a key issue on the Richards project that we need to discuss," is a standard communication tool. This tool is effective because the speaker clearly is taking responsibility for his or her view and at the same time is giving the other person the opportunity to consider whether or not he or she shares that view.

Taking responsibility is a great way to identify and clarify individual points in a discussion. If there is a downside to excessive use of "I" messages, it is the possibility that you may come across as overly self-referencing or egocentric in the discussion, and others may feel that you are not promoting team interaction.

Listening Actively

Active listening allows you to give the other person the message that you are hearing what he or she is saying (without necessarily agreeing with the point). An active listening comment may be, "Carl, I hear that you strongly believe that the project is not going to be done on time unless you get two additional engineers on the project." This response lets Carl know that you have heard his message, which is crucial to effective communication, but does not commit you to agreeing with his point.

Active listening is an effective tool to use when the other person has very strong feelings about something and needs to "get it off his or her chest" before continuing with the conversation. Active listening keeps the communication moving, allows your partner to be heard and understood, and buys you some time if you feel uncertain about how you want to respond to the issues being discussed. If over-used, however, active listening can have the negative effect of making you appear wishy-washy, patronizing, or perhaps unable to make a decision.

Asking Open-Ended Questions

Open-ended questions allow the answering party the chance to expand on a point without feeling forced to respond in the framework of a yes or no answer. Open-ended questions work well in situations where answers are not so clear-cut to warrant a yes or no answer. For example, assume that you are interested in finding out how a certain team member is handling a key aspect of the project. An open-ended question such as "Phil, would you please lead me through a description of what you've done recently on the project?" will elicit this type of information.

This question offers Phil latitude for responding, which will likely reduce his defensiveness and allow him to speak with a degree of comfort, because he is setting the direction. As the questioner, this style of questioning allows you to sit back and listen for responses to your key areas of interest.

If Phil fails to address one of your areas of interest, you can use a follow-up question such as, "Sounds good, but can you please tell me a little more about how you are covering the administrative details?" Open-ended questions help create an "expansive" tone in the conversation, encouraging your partner to volunteer more information.

What is the risk of using open-ended questions? The risk is coming across as indirect and unfocused, possibly having a hidden agenda or a concern that is not verbalized. To the more concrete individual, open-ended questions may seem nebulous.

Tracking the Message

All of us have had the frustrating experience of suddenly realizing that we are talking with someone about four different subjects at once and have no idea how we got off the topic.

This often occurs when both parties are not tracking the content or purpose of the discussion, and one or both members are inserting new topics into the discussion. This insertion of a new topic can occur for a number of reasons, including a failure to listen to the other party's key message, a strong emotional reaction by one of the parties, or a tendency to avoid closure on one subject before moving on to a new one.

An example of a tracking statement is: "Bob, I think we are going off topic. Let's back up to the point where you were mentioning the cost for the software package. I think that's the point where I started to lose you."

Reframing the Point

At times, discussions reach a point where communication is faltering or negative tones have infiltrated the exchange between people. Unless some change takes place, the discussion is headed for failure.

In these situations, a valuable communication tool is "reframing." Just as the picture framer puts a new frame around an existing painting and changes the tone of the painting, you can put a new "frame" around the failing discussion and create a new sense of optimism or achievement.

For example, let's assume that the team has been talking for 45 minutes about the lack of engineers needed to complete the software project on time and within budget. The tone in the room is one of frustration, with some sense of hopelessness and resignation. Reframing this discussion would be to put a different spin on the conversation, to see the issues from a different perspective—one that offers more optimism. A reframing comment at this point of the discussion could be something like: "Let's face it. If the discussion keeps going in this direction, we are not going to get anything done. What if we look at this situation as an opportunity to build a bridge between the engineering group in the other division and our group? We've said for a long time that a bridge like that would be good for us to have."

Reframing the issue, which can be done by any person in the conversation, involves creative thinking and a willingness to take a chance by offering a new perspective. When offering a reframing comment, be prepared for some people to remain stuck in the negative and to resist these creative alternatives. Be persistent. You may need to state the same reframing message in different ways before you achieve success.

IDENTIFYING AND APPRECIATING INDIVIDUAL DIFFERENCES: THE MBTI APPROACH

Obviously, teams are collections of individuals. To communicate effectively, it is crucial for the project manager to develop the ability to perceive the different personal styles on the team. The project manager will then be able to tailor communication approaches to the styles of the individual team members.

There are many ways to assess the style and personality of project team members. One conceptual framework that can be useful when considering individual differences is the Myers-Briggs Type Indicator (MBTI). Based on the work of Carl Jung (1971), the MBTI describes various components of personal styles. Jung believed that individuals vary in how they approach and perceive the world. In today's world of work, the MBTI is used extensively with teams, both as a team-building instrument and as a method for discovering the different communication styles present on a team (Hammer 1996).

The MBTI may be administered in a number of formats by certified practitioners. Some teams prefer to take the instrument via various online assessment forms; other teams prefer to take it in a shortened, hard copy form during team meetings.

In essence, the MBTI measures an individual's preferences among four pairs of qualities or preferences:

- *Extravert or Introvert.* The extraverted focus applies to individuals who get energized by a significant amount of interaction with the outside world. This type of individual enjoys an action orientation in life and becomes bored if things move too slowly.

In contrast, the introverted individual is energized by reflective activities away from lots of outside stimulation. This type of person enjoys being involved in tasks where they can really immerse themselves in the depth and the details of the issue.

- *Sensing or Intuition.* The person with a sensing preference looks at the world from a pragmatic, concrete, and immediate frame of reference. The sensing person prefers to use the five senses to attend to the world with a present-tense focus aimed at solving problems that can be scored, measured, or quantified.

  The intuitive person, on the other hand, prefers to look at a problem with more of a big-picture focus, eyeing future possibilities and trends. This person enjoys insights and abstract-based activities and has less interest in the concrete present than the sensing person does.

- *Thinking or Feeling.* The individual with a thinking-based decision-making style likes to look at the logical and rational components of the issue and make a decision that is supported by facts, analysis, and numbers.

  The feeling-based decision maker, in contrast, makes decisions "with the heart." The feeling person prefers to consider values, beliefs, and personal feelings—types of "information" that are much more subjective in nature.

- *Judging or Perceiving.* The person with a judging approach prefers to use an orderly approach to plan and structure activities and events. The judging person seeks to achieve closure on tasks and is generally quite goal-oriented.

  The perceiving person, conversely, wants to approach the world in a less structured manner, leaving things more to chance while displaying comfort with flexibility and responding to whatever comes up in the moment. Perceivers are often viewed as curious and willing to engage in many activities simultaneously.

COMMUNICATION TIPS: USING THE MBTI IDEAS TO DELIVER YOUR MESSAGE

By using the ideas on individual differences suggested by the MBTI, you can tailor your message to reach each of the unique styles on your team. By customizing your message, you increase your chances of successful communication and cooperation on the part of your team members. Table 3-1 is a summary

---

Table 3-1. Communication Tips Using the Myers-Briggs Preferences

Style of Individual	Compatible Type of Communication
Extraversion	Get together personally to think out loud.
Introversion	Help draw out this person, and then give them some time to privately reflect on your message.
Sensing	Present tangible facts, examples, data, and real-world experiences to make your point.
Intuition	Offer a "big picture" overview, presenting concepts that are crucial for your discussion.
Thinking	Present arguments that appeal to a rational analysis of the facts; appeal to the "head."
Feeling	Talk more from the "heart," using statements that address values and gut-level decision making.
Judging	Be orderly in presenting your message, and keep the discussion moving toward resolution and closure.
Perceiving	Allow for an open-ended discussion, staying flexible about the agenda.

of pointers from the MBTI that you can use to send your message to your project team members. (Additional thoughts and techniques for using the MBTI with project team members can be found in Flannes 1998.)

Communicating with the Extraverted Team Member

The extraverted team member is the person who is interactive, who focuses attention and energy outside him- or herself, who enjoys mixing with people, and who generally has a great deal of verbal contact with others. The extravert wants to be involved and to be at the center of the action.

To communicate effectively with an extraverted team member:

- Think out loud with this person; the extravert enjoys brainstorming.

- Communicate in a personal, face-to-face manner if possible, and minimize written, e-mail, or other types of communication that the extravert may view as too "impersonal."

- Place the extravert in settings where group communication is needed, such as brainstorming sessions; this type of milieu will stimulate the extravert and will get the creative juices flowing.

- Because extraverts can be verbally outgoing, they can dominate group meetings, particularly when dealing with more introverted team members. Work to keep the extravert's output in such settings at an acceptable level.

Communicating with the Introverted Team Member

Introverts are known for keeping a lower profile within group discussions, and they tend to be more thoughtful and reflective than expressive. They often appear deep in thought and may need some supportive prodding before they will offer an opinion.

When communicating with an introvert, consider the following:

- One-on-one settings often allow the introvert to be more disclosing and communicative. Within group settings, the introvert may remain quiet or less involved.

- Introverts do not particularly enjoy thinking out loud. Rather, they usually prefer to have an issue raised and then have some time to think the issue through before responding.

- Introverts may prefer more impersonal methods of communicating, such as e-mail or written documents. Such written messages give them the privacy they prefer to reflect and think something through before responding.

Communicating with the Sensing Team Member

The sensing person approaches the world with a pragmatic, tangible, and immediate focus, paying close attention to details while working at a steady pace. This person wants to deal with tasks in ways that can be quantified and measured.

When communicating with a sensing team member, consider the following approaches:

- Give the sensing person details, facts, examples, and concrete points. They have little use for theory or "the big picture."

- Stay in the present when delivering your message. Let them know the current importance of your message.

- Stick to the business at hand. The sensing person perceives extra communication about tangential matters as a distraction.

Communicating with the Intuitive Team Member

The opposite of the sensing person is the person who approaches the world through the style of intuition. The intuitive person likes to develop "the vision" and is good at synthesizing future possibilities and trends. Routine tasks are boring for this individual as he or she is always looking for better ways to do things.

To be successful when communicating with the intuitive style, consider these approaches:

- Provide a big picture of the issues and an overview of where you envision the discussion may take you. During the work of the project, discuss the goals and how the project supports the organization's vision.

- Remember that this style likes to theorize and follow different tangents during a conversation; you may need patience as this person brings up a number of other areas that may seem unrelated to the problem at hand.

- In project meetings, the intuitive person will often communicate with peers by assuming the role of devil's advocate, expressing ideas and messages that seem "outside the box" or tangential to the current point.

Communicating with the Thinking Team Member

As the name suggests, the person with a thinking style prefers to interact with the world in ways that are consistent with a thoughtful approach. Communication is often concise and to the point, focusing on a logical presentation of the facts. A rational mode of addressing a situation is adopted, and the thinking person is frequently observed as relating "from the head" when solving problems.

The best way to make your point with a thinking person is to:

- Present a logical argument, focusing on an analysis of the situation that is grounded in an assessment of the facts

- Get to the point; the thinking person has little interest in casual conversation

- Not take it personally if you encounter a thinking person with little need for small talk.

Communicating with the Feeling Team Member

The feeling person uses a significantly different approach from the thinking person when dealing with the world. The feeling person places emphasis on the subjective aspects of the situation, such as personal values, how people feel about the issue, and what the "gut" says is the correct thing to do.

Try these methods when communicating with the individual with a feeling style:

- Appeal to this person's values when making your argument.

- Expect this person to talk a great deal about feelings; he or she may put less emphasis or credence on the logical facts of a situation.

- Consider that this person may need to talk feelings through, or "get it off their chest," before they are able to move to verbal communication geared to tangible problem solving.

Communicating with the Judging Team Member

Judging refers to an approach in which the individual uses an orderly method to structure activities and endeavors. Judging people like to have a project plan, a detailed work breakdown structure, or an agenda for each project meeting. They are motivated toward gaining closure on an event and moving forward.

Because the person with the judging preference seeks order and structure, consider trying these approaches:

- Present your message in an orderly manner, using agendas and outlines to define the purpose of the discussion.

- Stay on point and try to avoid drifting into other topics or tangential points.

- Remember that this person works toward closure; keep the conversation moving toward a conclusion. Set both time and topic parameters before beginning.

Communicating with the Perceiving Team Member

The perceiving person prefers flexibility and spontaneity, and does well when multi-tasking. For the most part, perceiving people like to keep their options open and prefer not to work from a schedule or plan. Talking with this type of person will be a free-flowing experience with little need for structure and closure.

Consider these suggestions when working with a perceiving team member:

- Stay flexible and avoid using a rigid agenda for your meeting.

- Remember that this person will want to let the communication take its natural direction; expect that many topics may be mentioned and that the time of the meeting may seem open-ended.

- Gently help this person stay on track when required; offer comments that acknowledge his or her ideas but still help maintain focus.

PAYING ATTENTION TO THE TONE AND TEXTURE OF COMMUNICATION

Just as important as considering the individual styles and preferences of your team members as you begin to craft your communications is having a keen awareness of the texture and tone of any communication. This awareness involves:

- Being "present" during the discussion

- Listening to the "music behind the words"

- Considering the variables of alliance and context

- Keeping the communication on a reciprocal level

- Paying attention to the content and process aspects of a communication.

Being "Present" During the Discussion

Being in the present when communicating suggests a posture that places emphasis on the thoughts, ideas, feelings, and beliefs you are experiencing at that specific moment in the conversation. This is an awareness of your mood, energy level, and emotions. For example: Are you having a good day? Feeling angry?

Having this awareness does not mean that you have to disclose or act on these feelings when you are communicating. Rather, the goal is to have a healthy awareness about what is going on with you now, so you can use that awareness to communicate more effectively with your team members.

How can a project manager work on being present during a conversation? Here are two approaches to consider:

- *Reflect on your immediate feelings.* Your goal should be to develop an awareness of what you are feeling at that moment. Such an awareness will help you avoid stepping into potholes as you communicate with the other person.

- *Reflect on what your body is telling you.* This physical level of awareness is often a great source of "data," revealing what is going on with us. Each person usually has his or her own set of body cues that signal important information about what is going on emotionally at that moment.

An awareness of your feelings and your body cues will enable you to exhibit the following behaviors with your stakeholders:

- Effectively hear what the other person is saying to you.

- Demonstrate more respect and consideration for the other person

- Be more efficient in your decision making.

Listening to the "Music Behind the Words"

Buell encourages people to "listen to the music behind the words" (Flannes and Buell 1999). By this, he is challenging us to listen to the message that is rarely verbalized. This is the message that indicates mood and emotions. The obvious message, which often masks the "music," is frequently referred to as the content of the message and refers to the subject of the discussion. The music behind the message is the subtle affective level that tells you so much more about what is happening.

Consider this example of listening to the music behind the words:

Judith told her project manager that the project was meeting specifications, was under budget, and would be completed on time. The project manager heard these words, registered that Judith was saying that everything was in good shape, and then allowed the conversation to end.

However, if the manager had listened to the "music behind the words," he might have noticed her tone of voice, facial expressions, and body gestures. These indicators would have said, "I'm bored with this project, it's not challenging me, and I'm frustrated that you don't find something for me that is more to my skill level!"

By listening on this deeper level, the project manager would have picked up important cues suggesting that things were actually not going well on the project.

Considering the Alliance and the Context

It is not possible to describe the "right" thing to say in any given situation. The right thing to say is always a function of the nature of the alliance or relationship between the two people, plus an awareness of the context in which the communication is taking place.

Bugental (1990) developed the concepts of alliance and context. "Alliance" refers to the nature of the relationship. Different types of alliances exist between friends, between project team members and the project manager, between team members and outside vendors, and between strangers thrown together on a newly formed team. Each of these alliances differs in the degree of comfort, intimacy, openness, trust, shared history, and common goals. Being aware of the nature of the alliance offers the chance to tailor the communication to the intricacies and the specifics of the immediate relationship.

Examples of types of alliances include the following relationships:

- Two friends who have worked together for 12 years

- Two programmers, each new to the company, assigned to work for the first time with each other

- Two virtual team members, from different cultures, working together.

There is no ideal alliance. Each alliance needs to be seen as a "living thing," requiring nurturing and attention. Remember, every alliance is dynamic. Be careful not to take any alliance for granted.

- Alliance refers to the nature and quality of a specific relationship.

- Alliances differ in degrees of history, trust, openness, formality, and role.

Bugental's view of "context" addresses the idea that an effective communication is a function of an awareness of current circumstances. For example, in deciding how to tailor a message to a team member, the project manager should consider a number of context variables. These variables may include the current mood of the other person, the amount of pressure on the project team, or the fact that the organization may have recently undergone a reduction in force. A context variable will also include the setting: whether the message is being delivered in front of a formal group of project stakeholders or over lunch at a neighborhood cafe.

By being aware of the context in which you are speaking, you can craft messages that are conducive to the current surroundings, thus helping put the other person at ease and increasing the odds of delivering your message effectively.

When considering how to use the concept of context in communicating, be aware of these variables:

- Degree of formality or informality of the surroundings

- Current atmosphere in the workplace (e.g., anxiety, stress, pressing deadlines, recent reductions in force)

- Level of "intimacy" of the setting (e.g., individual, group setting).

Many of these ideas behind the concepts of alliance and context are obviously grounded in common sense. However, it is precisely because these ideas do appear to be common sense that we often overlook them or give them minimal consideration when we are communicating.

If we keep the concepts of alliance and context clearly in mind, and if we slow down and take time to apply them sensibly, we can achieve greater success in communication.

Keeping the Communication Reciprocal

Another important but subtle aspect of communication is the ability to create an atmosphere where people on the team are treated with mutual respect and dignity, regardless of the team member's seniority or level of expertise (Buber 1970). In essence, this way of communicating is communicating to the other as an equal, not "talking up" or "talking down."

Here are some ways the project manager can apply the idea of reciprocal communication to the day-to-day project setting:

- When looking at your communication partner, try to visualize this person as an equal.

- Try to view the exchange as being between two equal people talking about a problem or situation.

- Watch out for the natural tendency to treat people as stereotypes; such an approach locks one into rigid ways of seeing the other and creates long-term barriers to improved communications.

Being Aware of the Content and the Process

Any communication can also be viewed through the filters of "content" and "process."

Content refers to the subject that is being discussed, such as the results of the project review meeting, what someone had for lunch on Tuesday, or the hardware items in next year's budget. Content items are the obvious parts of a communication and are the aspects that people can usually track most easily.

The more complex aspect of a communication is the process, which refers to the manner, style, and methods in which the content is presented. Process focus looks at issues such as:

- Is one person dominating the discussion?

- Are people's comments coming across in critical or cynical styles?

- Does one person continually interrupt when a particular person is talking?

- Does one person get very quiet when conflict enters the discussion?

Process areas deal with the more intangible aspects of a communication; they often suggest an underlying feeling or emotional response that is not being expressed directly.

By paying attention to the process level of communication within the team, the project manager can identify unspoken issues, problems, or resistances that are hindering the progress of the project. Attending to process communication issues often takes some nerve and courage. Be active, assertive, and willing to speak your mind.

RECOGNIZING COMMUNICATION "STOPPERS"

We all fall victim to a number of communication shortcomings. The following four behaviors plague us from time to time, particularly when we are fatigued or when we feel emotionally threatened. Which of the four is your biggest risk area?

Denial

A little denial in life is not bad and can sometimes help us get through a tough time. However, denial works against us when we stubbornly maintain a view or position even when those around us continue to make strong arguments to the contrary. For example, we may continue to deny team members' messages that we are too controlling during team meetings, even after hearing this message four or five times.

To monitor your risk of falling into the trap of denial, consider the following suggestions:

- When communication continues to fail, ask an open-ended question, such as, "Am I missing something here that you are trying to tell me?"

- Stay receptive and non-defensive to feedback from such an open-ended question.

Projection

Projection is defined as attributing to others a feeling or belief that, in actuality, we hold ourselves. The negative aspect of projection is attributing a belief or attitude to another member of the team without confirming the reality of the projection for that team member. For example, if a project manager believes that all others on the team must share his or her specific view about how to approach a project design process, then this project manager is projecting his or her belief upon others.

Here are some ways to keep projection under control:

- If you think that others believe, think, or feel as you do, confirm it with them before you move forward, particularly on key issues.

- Use an "I" statement, followed by a question of inquiry. For example: "I believe very strongly that the specs for this project need to be re-evaluated and probably changed. Am I correct in assuming that you feel the same way?"

Displacement

Who has not had a fight with a family member one morning, and then come to work and chewed the head off of the first co-worker who said something to them?

Displacement occurs when some emotion or strong feeling that has been generated in one setting (in this case, the fight at home) gets "displaced," or passed on, to someone (in this case, the co-worker) who has done nothing to warrant such treatment. The innocent co-worker has no idea where this emotion originated and usually feels confused and untrusting toward the person who delivers the blow.

Strong feelings are often generated in the complex world of project management, where the project manager has many relationships to monitor and must navigate the tricky waters of matrix management and conflicting stakeholder agendas.

Under these circumstances, it is easy to displace feelings upon innocent third parties. However, there are steps a project manager can take to reduce the risk of displacement.

Here are some ways to minimize displacement:

- After an argument (or any interaction where negative feelings have been created), stop and take notice of what you are feeling.

- Before getting involved in another interaction (such as a meeting or discussion), take some time to let the negative feelings subside.

- As you begin the next interaction, do your best to initiate some "discussion with yourself," such as, "I'm still angry from the last meeting, but my anger is not about Joe, with whom I'll be meeting, so I need to go slow in our discussion."

These approaches to managing the risk of displacement can be surprisingly effective and can have profound influence on keeping communication succinct and straightforward. In a sense, these approaches to managing displacement are an evolution of the old advice to "count to 10 before speaking."

Objectification

Project work is difficult, with many people and many different types of relationships to manage. After a certain amount of experience and time struggling with different types of relationships, we can slip into the potentially risky habit of developing a "shorthand" to explain these different relationships to ourselves. Consequently, we create labels and categories such as "sponsoring executive," "project auditor," "outside vendor," and "project numbers guy."

These shorthand terms allow us to put people into categories so that we can relate to them more readily. We create assumptions about the nature of each of these categories, which helps us plan how to deal with the categories; in essence, these assumptions give us a blueprint for explaining how these people operate.

Viewed from a negative perspective, however, these categories become stereotypes. When we use these stereotypes in dealing with others, we run the risk of turning people into static categories or objects. When this takes place, objectification of the other person occurs.

Objectification of a project team member generally happens slowly. At some point, however, the objectification becomes solidified, and it becomes difficult to see people as they really are: dynamic, changing human beings who rarely conform to the boxes into which we often place them.

Guarding against the tendency to objectify is difficult. The best approach to reduce the risk is to be aware of your assumptions about a specific person or group. Here are some possible objectifying assumptions held by one project manager:

- Project auditors care only about the numbers.

- Auditors never listen to what I have to say concerning project budget overruns.

- They always start meetings with the rudest comment they can make.

If you notice that your list of assumptions contains words such as "only," "never," "they," and "always," then you can assume that you are starting to turn auditors into objects—entities with fixed and rigid qualities. Once the objectification begins, communication becomes problematic. Your messages to the auditors may get more stylized and rote, emanating from your stereotype of what constitutes an "auditor." Eventually, you start wearing a set of blinders that will not allow you to see any "auditor" communication and behavior that does not conform to your preconceived categories or expectations.

Every project manager can practice and improve communication skills. Small improvements in skill levels pay disproportionately big returns in terms of communication effectiveness. Keep in mind the following suggestions:

- *Pay attention to individual differences.* Team members will vary in terms of the most effective tool to use in getting your message across to them. An understanding of a system such as the MBTI can provide many ideas on how to tailor your messages to your particular team members.

- *Consider the issues of alliance (the nature of the relationship) and context (the setting in which the communication is taking place)* as you work to craft the most effective message.

- *Practice the "nuts and bolts" techniques* of communication. Experiment. Find your most effective tools. Get feedback from others about your success in trying out new behaviors.

- *Stay open to feedback about your blind spots.* Everyone has them, so try to receive that type of feedback without becoming defensive. This is not easy to do, but give yourself credit when you try.

- *Observe those who communicate well,* and adopt approaches from them that you think would work for you. Successful interpersonal communication is more art than science.

Discussion Questions

You have been the project manager on a telecommunications project for only four weeks, and already, you have experienced a number of communication problems on your team. Your frustration is mounting as you review what has happened to date:

1. Two of your senior engineers keep calling you into meetings with them because they cannot seem to communicate with each other and they want you to help them "sort things out."

   What approach would you take in trying to figure out why these people are not communicating effectively with each other?

2. You ask one of your team members to attend a meeting with a group of external stakeholders. After the meeting, you get a call from your counterpart on the stakeholder's team complaining about your team member's performance in the meeting. The other project manager yells, "This guy didn't hear a thing we said today!"

   What communication skill does this person seem to lack? How might you handle this situation?

3. You are puzzled that two of your most competent technicians never seem to say anything during project meetings, although they have many good ideas to contribute.

   What might be contributing to these people's silence during the meetings? What could you do to assist them in being more communicative during team meetings?

CHAPTER 4

The Art of Motivation

Motivating team members is more art than science. A good motivator can tailor an appropriate approach for each individual on the team.

Certain global workplace trends affect the ability to motivate team members. In the context of those trends, the project manager must adopt specific approaches to motivating each team member as well as the team as a whole. In adopting these approaches, the project manager should be aware of common motivation mistakes. Finally, a motivation checklist can help project managers work effectively with their teams.

GLOBAL TRENDS THAT AFFECT MOTIVATION

Three trends influencing the world of work make motivating team members challenging.

First is the ongoing reductions in force through outsourcing or offshoring of many key activities. Organizations in both the public and private sectors continue to downsize, with no end in sight. Nearly all downsizing results in situations where the surviving employees are required to "do more with less." Motivating team members in downsized organizations is difficult because the remaining employees experience feelings of anger and guilt (Noer 1993). In organizations or industries with repeated downsizings, it is not unusual to find pervasive cynicism and skepticism among the surviving employees.

Downsizing has led to the second trend that hinders motivation: a change in the unspoken employment contract between the company and the employee. The former assumption that good work leads to job security has been changed to an assumption only of getting paid for doing the job today, with no guarantees for the future. In essence, the company owns the job and the employee owns the career. In such an environment, the project manager needs to be creative and nimble in determining strategies for motivation.

The third trend complicating a project manager's ability to motivate is the emergence of cross-cultural influences and the virtual team. Cross-cultural teams bring a richness of team members from different backgrounds and viewpoints. However, this very richness involves a host of different "norms" for motivating team members across cultural groups and locations (Rad and Levin 2003).

STRATEGIES FOR MOTIVATING TEAM MEMBERS

Several strategies are available to the project managers for motivating team members.

Motivating Using Personal Style

In addition to being used for identifying individual differences on a team (as discussed in Chapter 3), the Myers-Briggs Type Indicator (MBTI) can be used to describe different sources of motivation for the various personality styles. The project manager with either formal or informal knowledge of team members' MBTI styles can use this knowledge to motivate individuals more effectively.

Table 4-1 (based on the work of Flannes 1998) presents information that the project manager can use to motivate the various members of the project team. For example, a successful motivational approach for the team member who has the extraverted and sensing MBTI preferences would be place to him or her with many people assigned to solve tangible and real-world problems. In contrast, the introverted person with intuition and

Table 4-1. Motivating Different MBTI Personality Styles

Personality Style	Best Approach to Motivating
Extravert Outgoing, enjoys dealing with people	Have this person focus on the relationship aspects of the project, such as meetings with stakeholders.
Introvert Quiet, reflective, inner-directed	Offer this person work that requires extended periods of concentration, possibly working alone.
Sensing Pragmatic, practical, down-to-earth	Give this person work that has a distinct completion point and can be measured in concrete terms.
Intuitive Conceptual, big-picture	Put this person to work on the strategic and design portions of the project, relating the project's objectives to the organization's strategic objectives.
Thinking Logical, analytical	Present this individual with tasks requiring quantitative skills, in-depth analysis, or research.
Feeling People-oriented	Allow this person to be in roles involving nurturing, supporting, and customer relationship management.
Judging Orderly, structured, timely	Permit this individual to create schedules, budgets, and project closure systems.
Perceiving Flexible, spontaneous	Direct this person toward situations requiring trouble-shooting.

thinking preferences would tend to be motivated by tasks that give him or her time to reflect individually on innovative possibilities involving an analytical and logical approach to decision making.

When using a personal style system such as the MBTI, it is important not to take the system too literally. Systems such as the MBTI are excellent for giving you a window to look through when thinking about motivation, but the best way to motivate someone is to ask them what motivates them—and to listen carefully to what they tell you.

Motivating Using Career Stages

People evolve through different stages in a career.

Schein (1990) presents a career stage model that involves ten distinct stages that a person goes through in a career, regardless of chronological age. An understanding of Schein's model can provide insights for a project manager into how to motivate team members.

Stage One and Stage Two occur in a person's life before entering the world of project work. These stages involve the early years of initial career exploration followed by formalized career preparation, such as college and specialized training.

Stage Three involves formal entry into the workplace, where real-world skills are acquired. To motivate a team member in this stage, give him or her a chance to demonstrate competency in a variety of tasks—to show the world they "know their stuff."

In Stage Four, training in the concrete application of skills and professional socialization takes place. The identity of being a professional is becoming established. Motivational approaches by the project manager will be most effective during this stage if they focus on assisting the team member in mastering the subtle technical and professional nuances of his or her profession.

During Stage Five, the team member has gained full admission into the profession based on demonstrated competency and performance. Project managers can be most effective during this period by using motivational methods that help team members perceive themselves as full-fledged, responsible contributors, possibly by assigning them to senior roles on the team.

Stage Six involves a sense of having gained a more permanent membership in the profession. To motivate a professional in Stage Six, offer opportunities for professional visibility, such as being a member of a cross-functional team or serving as a team advocate with other stakeholders.

Team members functioning in the final four stages require more motivational sophistication from the project manager, because the challenges and issues inherent in these stages are more complex and demanding.

Stage Seven involves the natural mid-career assessment or crisis. In this stage, questions are asked about the value of the career, what has been accomplished, and whether or not a new direction can be identified. The best way to motivate a person in Stage Seven is to focus on identifying new directions within the existing project that the team member could pursue, with the hope that the new direction creates a spark that translates into increased motivation.

Stage Eight involves the challenge of maintaining momentum as the career starts to move toward the end. Motivation during this stage and Stage Nine (when the individual begins to disengage from the profession and the world of work) involves:

- Helping the team member focus on a project task that he or she has yet to accomplish during his or her career.

- Helping the team member get excited about what sort of legacy he or she wants to leave in the company or within the profession. For example, the legacy could take the form of developing educational resources or coursework.

Stage Ten, the retirement or separation stage, involves the team member coming to closure with employment with the organization or membership in the profession. Strategies during this stage should be based on:

- Motivating the team member to retire in a personally positive manner, such as completing the last assignment at a high level of quality

- Helping the transitioning person package his or her professional skills in a post-retirement consulting or coaching role, if that is of interest to the team member.

Consider the concepts of these career stages as starting points, and then use interpersonal communication skills to ascertain specifically what is motivating for the particular individual.

Motivating Using Career Values

Schein (1990) also developed another approach to examining what work functions and work-related values motivate people.

Schein believes that:

- The more we understand our own values in specific areas, the better we are able to achieve work satisfaction

- Our motivation in the workplace will be greatest when we are pursuing tasks and functions that are consistent with our values.

Schein's research identified eight work-related values, which he describes as "career anchors." The word "anchor" relates to a fundamental activity that individuals perceive is important for them when they consider the aggregate of their skills, motives, and values. The eight anchors have important implications for motivation.

Technical-Functional Anchor

The professional with a strong interest in being a specialist in his or her profession is an example of the technical-functional anchor or value. This person has little interest in roles involving general management and takes great pride in being a skilled, expert practitioner of the trade.

To motivate a technical-functional team member:

- Create opportunities for this person to learn specialized skills.

- Reward this person through a professional or technical advancement track as compared to a general management or leadership track.

General Management Anchor

The team member with a general management anchor is highly motivated by situations in which leadership roles are available. This person seeks to ascend to consistently higher levels of organizational control and leadership, and has little need to remain a technical expert.

Motivate the team member with a general management anchor by:

- Providing opportunities to manage some aspect of the project

- Offering concrete forms of acknowledgment, such as monetary compensation, status and titles, and recognition by senior managers.

Autonomy and Independence Anchor

The autonomy-driven team member has a strong desire to do things according to his or her own approach, with little external structure. This person can be problematic in a team environment and is often perceived as not being a team player.

To motivate the team member with the autonomy-independence anchor:

- Place this person in work that emphasizes self-reliance.

- Keep the person out of roles that involve repeated group decision making or general managerial functions.

Security and Stability Anchor

This person poses motivational challenges for the project manager because this team member seeks continuity, a steady work environment, and job tenure (qualities that are at odds with the project environment). Challenging and innovative project roles hold little interest for this professional.

Motivating someone with a security-stability anchor involves:

- Placing this person in roles that are more traditional, such as that of the project control officer or project administrator

- Guiding this person toward projects that tend to be of long duration.

Entrepreneurial-Creativity Anchor

The entrepreneurially driven team member can be a source of pleasure or frustration for the project manager, depending on the nature of the project. This individual has the urge to continually use a personal vision to develop new business ventures. These people work best when they can innovate and create; they often become restless on project tasks that are routine or predictable.

Motivate the entrepreneurial team member by:

- Involving this team member in creating the project vision and getting the project off the ground

- Keeping this person away from project roles with narrowly defined duties

- Quickly moving this person to start-up aspects of new projects and ventures as the project completion stage arrives, not expecting this team member to be efficient in closing the current project.

Service Anchor

This person wants to be of service in a professional activity that has personal meaning associated with its completion. In the world of technical project work, for example, the biologist seeking a position with a company conducting environmental clean-up activities may demonstrate this career value.

To motivate the team member with a service anchor, place this team member in roles where he or she can:

- Provide "customer service" to other team members or to project stakeholders

- Troubleshoot situations where customer or client complaints require someone with a desire to help or to be of service.

Pure Challenge Anchor

Being motivated is rarely a problem for the pure challenge team member, assuming that this person is engaged in tasks and duties that consistently provide a chance to feel professionally stretched and challenged. This person is always looking for that new professional challenge to master.

Motivate the challenge-focused team member by:

- Talking with him or her at the start of the project about identifying professional activities that offer challenges

- Keeping him or her in mind for the potential disaster points in the project when a "hero" is needed to save the day.

Lifestyle Anchor

The lifestyle career value often involves a team member looking for balance between work life and personal life, believing that his or her professional work is not the sole focus of their life. This person may value the flexibility offered by flextime or telecommuting.

Motivate the lifestyle team member by providing opportunities to:

- Work on tasks that have clear starting and ending points and do not regularly expand into personal time

- Be involved in project functions that do not require a great deal of travel or relocation.

Schein's approach to viewing team members from a perspective of career anchors can be a helpful filter through which the project manager can view the members of the team. The project manager can then craft appropriate motivational strategies that reflect the overall pattern of anchors for any one person.

Motivating Using Situational Considerations

Maslow (1970) devised a theory of motivation based on the premise that people are motivated to satisfy various needs according to a hierarchy, with the most basic needs at the bottom of a "needs pyramid." When one need is satisfied, the natural thrust for the individual is to move to the next higher need level and to attempt to get that need satisfied.

Maslow's hierarchy of needs encompasses seven levels:

Level 1: Basic physiological needs, such as food and nour-ishment

Level 2: Security and safety needs, such as stability and survival

Level 3: Belonging needs, exemplified by affiliation or love

Level 4: Esteem needs, including achievement and recog-nition

Level 5: Cognitive needs, such as the expansion of person-al knowledge

Level 6: Aesthetic needs, exemplified by a search for beau-ty or order

Level 7: Self-actualization needs, illustrated by the realiza-tion of one's personal potential.

Maslow's hierarchy of needs can be applied in a situational mo-tivation environment by addressing the immediate work chal-lenges facing a team member. Flannes and Buell (1999) adapted Maslow's hierarchy and redefined the need levels using situa-tions frequently encountered in project work.

Their adapted hierarchy reflects the idea that the project man-ager must observe the dynamic situational variables to moti-vate team members effectively.

Level 1: Job Survival Needs
In this adapted Maslow model, Level 1 needs represent the ba-sic needs of the team member (as Maslow described the basic need for food and water), such as maintaining one's job during organizational reductions in force. Little else is on the mind of the team member during this period of ensuring basic survival.

The project manager can motivate an individual at the job survival level by:

- Providing the team member with project tasks whose completion and exposure increase the chances of job survival.

Level 2: Job Safety Needs

Needs at this level involve issues for the team member such as believing that he or she can "survive" in the organization over time, and that his or her project management career path extends past the current project.

To motivate a team member whose situational focus is at the job safety level, the project manager should:

- Think out loud with the team member, as appropriate, about long-term opportunities within the organization, involving the functional manager as appropriate in this discussion.

Level 3. Belonging and Affiliation Needs

The team member functioning at this situational level is motivated (in a similar manner as described earlier in the discussion of Schein's career stages) by a need for affiliation and feeling part of the organization.

To motivate a team member who is at this level of seeking affiliation:

- Provide opportunities to create professional relationships and liaisons within the company in which the team member can feel he or she is "part of the action."

- Encourage the team member to become involved in professional organizations.

Level 4: Esteem Needs

Being recognized for professional accomplishments and holding a high level of visibility within the professional community are examples of team member needs at this level. A motivational approach is to place a team member in situations in which the individual can appear "on center stage."

Motivate the person operating at the esteem level by encouraging him or her to:

- Present papers, write articles, or give talks within the organization or at professional conferences.

Level 5: Intellectual Challenge Needs

Within the project world, this situational motivational level is often demonstrated by the team member who has mastery of advanced professional competencies (similar to Schein's stage seven involving the mid-career lack of interest or motivation) and is looking for something new to do.

Motivate the team member seeking intellectual stimulation by:

- Allowing him or her opportunities to learn more about the project world on a macro level, such as becoming more involved with tasks that demonstrate how this project integrates financially with other company strategic initiatives.

Level 6: "Aesthetic" Needs

Aesthetic needs in project management can be represented by a team member's interest in shifting from the "hard skills" of the profession to development of the "soft skills" that can be applied in project work, such as a senior project manager who has "seen it all" and now wants to give something back to the profession.

Motivate the team member interested in developing soft skills by encouraging him or her to:

- Become an informal mentor to a junior team member

- Serve as an informal customer relationship manager over the course of the project.

Level 7: Self-Actualization Needs

The hallmark of this situational stage is the individual whose comfort and sense of security allow him or her to take a path that is personally rewarding in terms of living up to their full potential. For some team members, this could mean a decision to leave the technical side of the organization and take a position, for example, within the organization's training department, designing training curriculums for entry-level technical staff.

There are few concrete steps a project manager can take to motivate a team member at this level, as the activities that motivate individuals are often less tangible than the day-to-day tasks of a project. Nevertheless, the project manager can:

- Encourage the team member to identify aspects of the current team project where he or she can "give back" or leave behind a personally meaningful achievement.

As a means of illustrating the situational variables that can affect team member motivation, we have taken some liberties in presenting this modified Maslow hierarchy. We have presented this model, however, to illustrate that a team member may move in a fluid manner, up and down, from one level to another, based upon the external, situational variables that he or she encounters during the course of a project.

For example, a team member may be operating from the esteem level (working to expand his or her professional network within the organization), but then may quickly drop to the survival level upon learning that company layoffs are planned and his or her job is at risk. Consequently, when using this adapted model of motivating team members, it is crucial for the project manager to remember that people and their needs are dynamic. External, situational variables such as downsizing, transfers, and project problems alter a person's immediate source of motivation.

SYSTEMIC APPROACHES TO MOTIVATING THE TEAM

In addition to pursuing strategies to motivate the individual members of the project team, the project manager should implement macro-level methods aimed at motivating the team as a whole. These systemic methods include:

- Creating an empowered, trust-based team

- Applying a team force-field analysis.

Creating an Empowered Team

Meredith and Mantel (2003) offer a project management application of a group motivation strategy in which team members experience a strong sense of empowerment through participatory management.

Empowerment, for Meredith and Mantel, is a participatory management approach that stresses:

- Individual initiative

- Solution creation and accountability

- The opportunity to be self-determinative in creating the structure and methods used to achieve project goals.

The challenge for the project manager who wants to lead in an environment highlighted by empowerment is walking that fine line between allowing decisions and direction to emerge from within the group and retaining the necessary leadership controls and monitoring over the project variables of performance, time, and cost. After the project manager and the team establish this fine line, the project manager needs to motivate the team in a manner that is based on trust among all team members.

Verma (1997) states that trust is a basic condition for the achievement of highly functioning project teams. By implication, establishing trust becomes a basic component of any successful project leader's strategies for motivating team members. Verma suggests that trust is developed, in part, by:

- Modeling desired behaviors, such as respect and the discussion of sensitive issues

- Helping create an atmosphere of interaction and friendly relationships

- Developing "win-win" strategies for individual and group goals.

Verma believes that team motivation is likely to flourish in groups that possess the following qualities:

- Pride, loyalty, and teamwork

- Self-discipline and accountability

- Dedication, credibility, trust, and dependability.

Applying Force-Field Analysis

Lewin (1948) explored forces within groups that support change and forces that inhibit change. Lewin believed that in any system (or group), both forces exist simultaneously to different degrees, depending on the unique conditions of the particular group. His model, called a force-field analysis, has been elaborated on and modified to meet the needs of motivating teams to perform and make changes. Packard (1995), for example, describes it as an effective tool for managers to use when instituting changes within the group or team. Force-field analysis can be a positive tool for project managers to use in examining the forces influencing motivation within a project team.

When defining the forces that hinder motivation, the project manager is actually dealing with individual and systemic forces that can be described as "resistances." Resistance to change, action, or motivation is to be expected and should not be labeled by the project manager in overly negative terms. In actuality, some resistance is often warranted, such as when a project manager is attempting to motivate team members to take an action that may not make sense or may even be wrong.

When encountering resistance, it is important for the project leader to:

- Question whether or not the resistance is grounded in a valid and accurate assessment of the current facts

- Make certain that the goals and benefits of the project have been clearly communicated to the team members

- Examine whether an issue of individual differences (such as a personality clash) is obstructing project cooperation and task buy-in.

MOTIVATIONAL MISTAKES

The project manager should experiment with different approaches to motivating team members, but should also be aware of motivational efforts that do not serve the cause of creating a motivated team environment. Here are some well-intentioned, but nevertheless questionable motivation strategies and beliefs:

- *"Whatever motivates me will motivate others."* This belief is an extension of the assumption that others want to be treated the way we would like to be treated. People are often motivated by the same approaches, but not always. Do not make assumptions about what will motivate someone—ask them!

- *"People are motivated primarily by money."* Although obviously valid on many levels, this belief does not explain the full range of human motivation. People are also highly motivated by personal acknowledgments from the manager, meaningful recognition from peers, and the opportunity to work in a setting in which they can keep developing marketable skills.

- *"Team members love to receive formal awards."* Clearly, many people value the opportunity to receive a formal award noting a special achievement. Frequently, however, formal awards are presented in a way that may actually cause employee cynicism, such as a situation where employees believe that the recipient of the award is chosen for reasons other than accomplishment, such as company politics or political correctness. Formal awards are likely to be motivating forces when team members themselves vote for the recipient, and when the award is not created as a means of masking some other issue.

- *"Give them a rally slogan."* Slogans can help gain initial team member focus and purpose, but their overuse can quickly backfire on the project manager. Slogans can turn the message behind the slogan into a sham; the overuse of slogans can have a patronizing effect on many self-directed professionals.

- *"The best project leader is a strong cheerleader."* Cheerleading is an important part of managing people, but the project leader needs to be careful not to overdo it. Cheerleading comments can be positive, but they need to be used carefully. Often, the best way to motivate people is to let them come up with the inspiration and energy for their own actions, free from outside cheerleading.

- *"These people are professionals. They don't need motivating!"* Project professionals are generally self-motivating, following an inner drive that leads to achievement and productivity. However, nearly everyone profits from occasional outside sources of motivation, particularly on projects that are lengthy or frustrating.

- *"I'll motivate them when there is a problem."* This approach to motivation takes the old adage that says "No news is good news" to an extreme. Unfortunately, people tend not to tell others when motivation is starting to suffer; the level of motivation usually needs to get seriously low before most people speak up and address the issue. The skilled motivator takes a proactive approach to motivating the team, not waiting for motivation issues to surface.

- *"I'll treat everyone the same. People like that, and it will be motivating for them."* It is safe to assume that it is important to treat everyone the same on issues of basic fairness and job performance standards. But, it is also important to recognize team members as individuals, especially when creating strategies to motivate each of the individuals on the team. Different things motivate people at different points in their lives.

MOTIVATIONAL CHECKLIST FOR THE PROJECT MANAGER

Here are four checkpoints to follow when considering how to motivate a team member:

1. Determine the team member's personal style (using the MBTI system or another framework for describing individual differences).

2. Assess the member's career stage (as described by Schein).

3. Identify the team member's career anchors (the work-related values described by Schein).

4. Remember to be proactive in motivating while keeping your motivational mistakes to a minimum.

Motivating team members is one of the most challenging and sophisticated "people" tasks required of the project manager.

In developing and implementing motivation strategies, the project manager should consider macro-level factors such as downsizing and sociological forces such as the increase of cross-cultural influences and virtual teams.

Motivational approaches must also consider team member variables such as personal style determinants, personal values, and career development stage, as well as situational variables.

The project manager should remember that all sources of motivation are fluid and dynamic. Keep in touch with team members to determine what is currently motivating for them. The best approach to use when deciding what is motivating for any particular team member is to ask that person. That may sound simplistic, but it will provide the project manager with a wealth of current, specific information that cannot be obtained through any other method.

Discussion Questions

Angelica is the project manager for a software development project. When she was given the role of project manager for this project, her manager told her that her team comprised some highly skilled professionals representing diverse backgrounds and professional goals.

These team members, the manager explained, "would need to be skillfully motivated to get the work completed on time."

As Angelica left her initial meeting with her manager, she started reflecting on how she would motivate these people, particularly given the rumor of impending company layoffs. She knew what things were motivating for her, and she assumed that these same things would also be motivating for the team members.

However, as she learned more about the specific backgrounds of her team members during her next meeting with her manager, she began to have second thoughts about what motivating approaches she could use successfully with these team members. One of the members, for example, was a long-term, introverted employee, 14 months from retirement. Another team member was a new employee who recently entered this country after completing his degree in another country. Two others were technical contractors "on loan" to the project for undetermined lengths of time. There was a disgruntled, mid-career engineer who believed that he should have been selected as project manager. Finally, two other team members were young, fast-track engineers who were noted for their technical innovation but were often perceived to be short on task follow-through.

Reviewing the composition of her team, Angelica realized that she would be significantly challenged to motivate each of these individuals given their unique situations and professional needs.

1. If you were this project manager, how would you motivate each of these different individuals?

2. What would be your first step in this process?

3. How would you assess your effectiveness?

CHAPTER 5

Managing Project Conflict

Conflict is inevitable in the project management world because projects involve a myriad of different stakeholders, including the team members, the client, the sponsoring organization, suppliers, and the interested public (Meredith and Mantel 2003). Conflict must be addressed if a project team is to operate effectively, and it can often have benefits for a project.

It is essential for project managers to understand the reasons underlying conflict on teams, the process by which an individual experiences conflict, what happens when conflict is not addressed, and the specific conflicts inherent in different project stages. A conflict resolution model developed by Thomas and Kilmann (1974) offers a useful approach that project managers can follow to resolve many conflict situations.

CONFLICT IS PERVASIVE

The reasons for conflicts on project teams are varied, relating to the intricacies of personalities and the systemic challenges of completing tasks within complex and challenging environments. Every organization and industry has conflicts. They are simply part of the price of doing business, and the project manager should consider both their positive and negative aspects (see Table 5-1).

There are many sources of conflict within a project team or organization. Systemic sources of conflict include conflicting loyalties and alliances, such as when a project team member works for both the project manager and a functional manager.

Table 5-1. Positive and Negative Aspects of Conflict

Positive Aspects of Conflict
- Productively challenges existing beliefs or paradigms
- Reduces the risk of intellectual compliance within the team ("group think")
- May create an opportunity to forge more effective team relationships and revitalize team energy and bondedness

Negative Aspects of Conflict
- When not addressed in a productive manner, can de-motivate team members and increase interpersonal withdrawal
- Decreases interpersonal communication, increases cynicism
- Adversely affects initiative and the willingness to take risks

---

Conflicts also arise following reductions in force, when the surviving employees struggle to obtain resources and personnel. Conflicts can also arise at the end of a project, especially when a "projectized" organization (in which project team members report directly to the project manager as they work full-time on the project) has been formed, and team members do not have a functional "home" as they await a new assignment.

Individual sources of conflict at work are also varied. These can include:

- Two team members may constantly irritate each other for no reason other than that their personalities are so different.

- Poor communication abilities can create chronic sources of worker conflict.

- Other conflicts emanate from the employee who brings acute personal problems (e.g., family problems, substance abuse) into the workplace.

- Conflicts can relate to the natural, different perspectives held by team members who were originally trained in different disciplines.

Conflict is not always a bad thing for a project, however. In actuality, conflict can serve a positive function on the team, becoming the energy that loosens the adhesive of old ideas.

When the project manager embraces and processes conflict in a constructive manner:

- An intellectually stimulating environment is created as team members challenge paradigms and constructs, pushing performance to higher levels.

- "Group think" is avoided as team members challenge status-quo approaches to solving problems.

- Opportunities are created to forge improved working relationships and to revitalize team energy.

THE PERSONAL EXPERIENCE OF CONFLICT: BODY AND MIND

The experience of conflict involves three distinct and often sequentially encountered levels of experience: cognitive, physiological, and affective (see Table 5-2).

The Cognitive Level

The cognitive level of conflict comes into play when a person notices that his or her "self-talk" contains themes of possible upcoming or current disagreement or conflict. For example, a project manager meets with a functional manager to discuss the resource assignments for an upcoming project. The project manager takes his seat in the functional manager's office and quickly realizes that the conversation is not going very well. Soon the project manager notices that he is having apprehensive thoughts such as:

"I hope she is more flexible than last time. I had to fight for every person I got from her staff for my last project. I'm going to blow my top

Table 5-2. The Experience of Conflict

Type of Conflict Experience	Signs and Symptoms
Cognitive level	Internal self-talk with themes suggestive of impending or current conflict states
Physiological level	Awareness of body cues such as increased heart rate, decreased respiration, tightening of muscles, desire to "fight" or "flee"
Affective level	Cognitive and affective cues being interpreted as indicating emotions such as fear, anger, and anxiety

if she gives me one of those excuses about how busy her department is. This meeting is going to go nowhere, just like last time."

These self-statements need to be closely monitored; if they are grounded in faulty assumptions, they must be internally challenged. Challenging a self-statement can take the form of creating another statement that is more neutral or positive, such as:

"Well, maybe this time we will find a way to talk about the subject in a more positive and professional manner. I'll do what I can to achieve that result."

In essence, the project manager needs to remember that neutral or positive self-talk helps reduce the length and intensity of the conflict and creates opportunities for improving relationships.

The Physiological Level

If negative self-talk themes continue during a discussion, then the experience of the conflict can move to the physiological level. An individual will notice bodily experiences such as a racing heart, sweaty palms, and problems with concentration.

As these physical conflict cues surface, the body begins to activate the autonomic nervous system (ANS), the subsystem of the central nervous system that is responsible for regulating and monitoring many involuntary bodily functions. Operating within the ANS is the sympathetic nervous system, which prepares the body for emergency physical and survival action, such as personal defense and protective aggression (e.g., fleeing from a perceived threat).

Once the conflict reaches this level of physiological activation, it is difficult for the individual involved to calm down and return to a less agitated level of functioning. To address conflict when it has reached the physiological level, the project manager needs to identify some form of active, internal self-monitoring that is focused on quieting the activated autonomic system (such as a calming self-talk statement or deep breathing).

The Affective Level

The affective level of the conflict experience involves the conscious experiencing of all the emotions associated with conflict: fear, anxiety, vulnerability, and anger. As these emotions become more acute, discomfort rises, usually within both individuals. The volume of the conversation increases, rhetoric becomes more ragged and less focused, and emotions play a greater role in individual decision making. When the experience reaches this level, the best thing the project manager can do is to create some form of time-out (e.g., reschedule the meeting, talk about less intense issues) and let emotions cool down.

WHEN CONFLICT IS NOT ADDRESSED

The natural tendency of most people, whether in work or personal situations, is to avoid conflict. After all, who wants to be involved in unpleasant interactions? If conflict in the project environment is not addressed, however, unfavorable outcomes will likely develop:

- People will withdraw from each other and retreat into individual spheres of influence, allowing issues to fester.

- Team member motivation and initiative will decrease, while cynicism will increase.

- Role rigidity will be fostered, with team members becoming inappropriately territorial about their functions and not exchanging information or assistance.

CONFLICT IN PROJECT PHASES

While many variables contribute to project conflict, prime contributors are the people, tasks, and sequential challenges inherent in the various stages of the project life cycle. The project manager should be aware of the potential sources of conflict found in each project stage.

Project Initiation Phase

In the initial phase of the project, the project manager attends to all aspects required to begin a major piece of work. Tasks include identifying key resources or required personnel, determining project success criteria, specifying required technology, and clarifying roles and responsibilities as well as policies and procedures.

As Meredith and Mantel (2003) state, it is crucial for the project manager, during the initial phase of the project, to encourage everyone to address conflict openly. Team members take their cues from the project leader at this formative stage. If the project manager is sending the message that conflict should be avoided, then team members will respond accordingly. This is particularly true when the team members are more junior or when they have a diminished sense of their own self-concept or competencies.

During the initiation phase, the project manager can establish a good precedent for handling conflict by serving as an example, role-modeling conflict resolution behavior early and often, and reinforcing that behavior in team members.

Project Planning Phase

One of the main challenges for the project leader during the project planning phase is developing relationships with key stakeholders such as the supporting functional managers. As all project managers can attest, the relationship with the functional manager can be fraught with complexities as the project manager attempts to gain the needed support of funds and personnel.

Working with the functional manager presents many opportunities for conflict. The project manager must clearly think through the needs, priorities, and motivations of the functional manager—which may be very different from those of the project manager—as fully and as carefully as possible.

During these times of relationship building, the functional manager may attempt to resolve a conflict by claiming to be the "technical" expert while indirectly casting the project manager in the less technically sophisticated role of a "generalist." For the project manager, it is best not to confront such an approach directly, since the functional manager will likely react defensively. The best approach is for the project manager to let those comments pass and to stay persistently focused on project needs. The project manager would be well advised simply to acknowledge the functional manager's competency in the technical area and keep the discussion moving forward.

In summary, the project manager needs to remember that the functional manager may have different needs and a different agenda. The best approach is to try to understand those needs and address them as directly as possible.

Project Execution Phase

During the project execution phase, the main activities of the project are underway and the bulk of the work is taking place. In terms of project content, key issues during this stage include unexpected problems, delays, technical problems, risks, or other unforeseen complexities possibly related to stakeholder expectations.

On the personal level, many of the situations involving conflict during this phase relate to issues of performance stress and perhaps even the unrealized personal "dreams" of individual team members.

When faced with a situation where a team member is disgruntled because he or she is not achieving a personal goal on the project, the project manager can respond by using the following tactics:

- Openly acknowledge with the team member that his or her personal goals may not be addressed during this project.

- Discuss with the team member whether any new personal goals could be established for the remainder of the project that would increase his or her motivation.

Project Closeout Phase

The closeout phase of the project presents special challenges for the project manager. Team members are often emotionally and intellectually fatigued. The pressure to complete tasks against time and resource limits has diminished personal resiliency. Team members may be experiencing uncertainty about their next assignments, which can create distraction. Additionally, the emotional disengagement from the team and the project can bring up issues of loss for certain team members, hampering productivity.

The project manager should be sensitive to these potential sources of conflict when driving the group toward project completion and closure.

During the closeout period, the project manager can be helpful by:

- Assuming that each team member may be a little "ragged" and not at full emotional or intellectual strength

- Paying individual attention to each team member, noting the best ways to help each team member flourish during this trying period.

THOMAS-KILMANN MODEL OF CONFLICT RESOLUTION

The Thomas-Kilmann Conflict Mode Instrument (TKI) is a self-assessment tool based on work in conflict resolution by Thomas and Kilmann (1974). This instrument helps the user define his or her primary and secondary conflict resolution styles as a competitor, an accommodator, an avoider, a compromiser, or a collaborator. Many team members have found this instrument helpful in obtaining quick and easy feedback regarding their preferred conflict resolution approach.

Usually, an individual develops comfort and competency in using one of these five conflict resolution approaches—and then overuses that approach even in situations when one of the other four approaches would be more productive. Thomas and Kilmann's model encourages us to:

- Develop skills in each of the five approaches

- Develop the ability to know when to use each approach.

Each of the five TKI approaches to resolving conflict is valid under certain circumstances. The challenge for the project manager is to know when to use each approach.

Competing

The "competing" approach to resolving conflict is grounded in a combination of being both assertive and uncooperative. This approach is often driven by a need for power, with individual concerns and goals pursued at the expense of others. It can be useful in specific situations in which unpopular actions must be taken, in a fast-paced environment, and on tasks when an individual is certain that his or her position is correct.

While competing may be effective in certain situations, it must be used judiciously and not as a primary tool. When competing is applied in the wrong setting, it can stalemate the conflict, alienate the other stakeholders, prevent the views of the other individual from being heard, and cause team members to lose sight of the overall goals and objectives of the project.

Before using the competing approach to conflict resolution, a project manager should:

- Attempt to use other less confrontational approaches

- Consider the long-term effects on ongoing working relationships with all stakeholders.

Here is an example of a competing statement that a project manager can use when the situation warrants:

"Bill, I understand that you want to do it your way, but I can't OK that change. We'll have to follow the existing document."

Avoiding

Avoiding works well in situations where the issue at hand is trivial, where there is little chance of winning, where more information or data are needed, or when interactions are emotionally heated and some form of cooling off period is warranted.

Avoiding can be harmful, however, when it results in unnecessary delays for the project or when it hinders communication. Moreover, the "avoiding" person runs the risk of being perceived by others as too passive.

Before applying the avoiding approach to conflict, the project manager should:

- Determine whether the issue is crucial or trivial to the project

- Assess the risk of possible project delay

- Consider the effect on personal reputation and the perception of others.

An example of an avoiding statement is:

"I realize that's an issue . . . let's leave it for now and get back to it next week."

Accommodating

The accommodating individual displays a high degree of cooperation but is low on assertiveness. Often, the focus for the accommodating person is on meeting the needs of the other person, occasionally at the expense of his or her own appropriate agenda.

The accommodating approach to conflict management can be helpful in demonstrating the quality of open-mindedness, particularly during the early, formative stages of the project team. Preserving harmony is another reason for using accommodation, as well as the need to avoid pointless competition over insignificant points.

When used to an extreme, however, accommodation can severely undercut a project manager's standing in the eyes of team members and other important stakeholders. The project manager who overuses accommodation may be viewed as weak and ineffectual, and may risk anger from team members who believe that their positions and needs are not being pursued forcefully.

When considering the conflict resolution approach of accommodation, the project manager should first answer the following questions:

- Is accommodation too much a part of my character, something that I use too often?

- Will my team react negatively to the use of accommodation?

- What are the long-term implications for my reputation in the organization if I use accommodation?

An example of an accommodating statement is:

"That's fine . . . we can do it whatever way you want."

Collaborating

The collaborator is the team member who emphasizes both assertiveness and cooperation and is willing to consider the merits of the other person's position. This approach is based on an attempt to combine the best of both individuals' positions into an integrated solution. Positive applications of collaboration include situations in which both positions are, to some degree, important and viable. Collaboration works particularly well in those instances where insights from both perspectives are valid, such as on projects that are culturally diverse.

The negative aspect of collaboration involves those circumstances where the integrated solution (i.e., the collaboration) results in a work product that is faulty because some of the integrated points were incorrect. Other pitfalls of collaboration involve situations where the desire to collaborate hinders the need to act quickly, such as during a project crisis.

The project manager should address these questions when considering collaboration:

- Are both positions really important and accurate, warranting a collaborative approach?

- Will the resulting product warrant the extra time that a collaborative approach requires?

An example of a collaborating statement is:

"That's a good idea . . . I hadn't thought of that. Let me tell you about my idea, and let's see if we can somehow combine them."

Compromising

In the compromise approach to conflict resolution, both individuals give a little and try to find middle ground. Compromise sounds similar to collaboration but differs in that it is more short-term oriented and is used productively in situations when temporary agreements need to be reached quickly. As with collaboration and accommodation, the project manager who uses compromise runs the risk of being perceived as too willing to give in to the other side or too willing to give up on his or her original position.

Use compromise when the following conditions are present:

- A short-term action needs to be taken quickly, and the compromise may not be of great significance.

- A need exists to demonstrate openness and flexibility.

An example of a compromising statement is:

"OK, I can change the completion date . . . but I'll need you to alter the amount of funding I'm getting."

CONFLICT RESOLUTION CHECKLIST

The following checklist for addressing a conflict covers four main areas:

1. Determining the project phase

2. Considering a possible lack of information

3. Assessing whether functional issues are present

4. Determining whether personality issues are present.

Consider the following points and questions to resolve a conflict in the most productive way.

1. What is the current phase of the project?

Each project phase has unique sources of conflict (Thamhain and Wilemon 1975):

- *Project initiation.* Conflicts are possible because of issues of project priorities, administrative procedures, and schedules.

- *Project planning.* Conflicts are possible because of priorities, schedules, and procedures, in addition to issues with functional managers and general personality disputes.

- *Project execution.* Schedules, technical challenges, and staffing issues are often sources of conflict.

- *Project closeout.* In addition to schedules, a primary source of conflict can be a clash of personality styles (that may be due to job stress and fatigue) and staffing (uncertainties regarding the next assignment).

With an awareness of the phase of the project and the type of possibly inherent conflict, the project manager can maintain the perspective needed to respond with the proper intervention.

2. Is the conflict the result of a lack of information or knowledge?

Many times, project conflict is due to a lack of information resulting from inadequate communication among stakeholders. Make sure all important information (both factual and "personal") is communicated to stakeholders. Such efforts at keeping the communication flowing are especially crucial when working with virtual teams.

3. Is the source of the conflict functionally based?

Functionally based conflicts arise between project managers and functional managers and between the project team (or the organization) and an outside party-at-interest (such as the customer, a subcontractor, or the public).

The project manager can minimize the risk of conflict with functional managers by understanding their needs and concerns. For example, if the organization is undergoing downsizing and if managers are rewarded when staff are fully used, the project manager can point out to the functional manager that the upcoming project will ensure that certain people on the functional manager's staff will be fully employed. Collaborative approaches should be considered in resolving conflict with functional managers.

4. Is the conflict personality-based?

Personality-based conflicts include clashes of personal styles, such as two people with "competitive" styles dealing with each other.

Conflicts caused by personal style can be understood through the MBTI system of viewing individual differences (presented in Chapter 3). Kirby, Barger, and Pearman (1998) present an excellent description of the frequent sources of conflict among the different MBTI preferences.

They suggest that, to resolve conflicts between an extravert and an introvert, remember that:

- Extraverts often approach situations at a brisk pace, frequently challenging subjects as they "think out loud."

- Introverts prefer a "measured pacing" of the discussion, preferring to maintain a more narrow focus.

Resolve conflicts between the sensing-oriented person and the intuitive-oriented person by remembering that:

- The person with the sensing style seeks to define the problem, or conflict, in the present tense, using concrete and measurable examples.

- The intuitive-oriented person will gravitate toward defining the conflict in broader terms, along the lines of concepts and trends rather than events and details.

Resolve conflicts between the thinking person and the feeling person by remembering that:

- The thinking person needs facts and analysis to come to resolution and is looking for the "correct" solution.

- The feeling person prefers to examine the underlying emotions held by the key participants in the conflict. Until these issues are explored to some degree, the feeling person has little interest in moving forward to a resolution.

To resolve conflicts between the judging person and the perceiving person, keep in mind that:

• The judging person prefers to move in a structured and deliberate manner toward resolution and closure of the conflict.

• The perceiving person may hesitate to agree on a resolution to the conflict based on the belief that there may be some better solution that has not yet been considered.

By developing a working understanding of the MBTI styles of the individuals involved in conflict, the project manager can develop a strategy that addresses the conflict resolution needs of the different styles and preferences.

MANAGING AGREEMENT: AS IMPORTANT AS MANAGING CONFLICT

As discussed in terms of the Thomas-Kilmann model, conflict can be resolved through various forms of "agreement," such as accommodation, collaboration, and compromise. One potentially negative aspect of these agreement-based strategies, however, is the risk that necessary team conflict may be overlooked, resulting in less optimal solutions coming to the forefront. The project manager may be viewed as performing an inadequate job of "managing agreement" on the project team when appropriate conflict is not brought to the surface by the team members.

Excessive agreement, accomplished in an effort to avoid conflict and not to offend, has been described by Harvey (1988) as a phenomenon labeled the Abilene Paradox. In this paradox, people within groups often do things that they really do not want to do just to avoid a conflict.

Team members and project managers can easily fall into the trap of excessive agreement. People within groups can assume a mentality of group think, in which unwritten group norms are created regarding how tasks should be accomplished. These unwritten rules of behavior (in this case, the need to agree with the project manager or with other team members as a means of demonstrating support) become established and codified as a result of team members taking performance cues from the behavior of the team leader.

Under circumstances of group think, team members may withhold disparate points of view because they are concerned about being viewed as "not a team player." When this withholding of contrary views reaches a certain level, members become disengaged, motivation wanes, and innovation suffers. The need to "agree" keeps the project moving forward, but often at the expense of the quality and sophistication of the project work.

How can the project manager manage the risk of having too much agreement on the team? The following are some ideas to consider:

- Observe and understand closely your own approach to conflict resolution. Are you an accommodator? A compromiser?

- Consider whether you reward or show some type of favoritism toward team members who follow your unspoken requests for "agreement."

- Sensitize the project team during its kickoff meeting to the dynamics of the Abilene Paradox and encourage team members to guard against it. Create an environment for the team in which "forewarned is forearmed." This process should be combined with development of a team charter laying out ground rules for the team that include guidelines for open and honest communication on matters of conflict.

Conflict surfaces for a variety of reasons, such as the challenges and pressures of the different phases of a project and the personalities of the various team members. Conflict is a natural aspect of any project team. Ideally, conflict surfaces within the project team in a manner that serves to create an intellectually challenging and stimulating setting.

Addressing conflict in an active fashion is a key requirement for the successful project manager. Left unattended, conflict impedes the development of effective interpersonal relationships among team members.

Conflict can be resolved through a number of approaches, including competition, avoidance, accommodation, collaboration, and compromise. Each of these five approaches to conflict resolution can be effective, assuming the approach is appropriate for the situation at hand.

To be successful in resolving the conflicts that are inherent in any project team, the project manager needs to first be aware of his or her own preferred approach to resolving problems. This self-awareness serves as the foundation from which the project manager can make necessary adjustments when working with the styles of the other team members.

Managing agreement is also a challenge for the project manager, as too much agreement on a team often masks conflict and hinders an honest exchange of disparate ideas, which can lead to creative and innovative project solutions.

Discussion Questions

1. Consider the following situation:

A project manager in an aerospace company was placed in charge of a multidepartmental team directed to work with another company to develop a product targeted for the growing recreational market. Each company had recently undergone significant layoffs, and the mutual goal was to use this new joint project as a means of developing greater viability for both organizations.

The project manager, aware that team members from both companies were still stunned from the recent layoffs, tried to adopt a posture that would address these sensitivities. Mistakenly, the project manager decided to try to act toward the team members in a way that they "would remain positive and not lose their motivation."

During the first several project team meetings, the project manager minimized conflicts between the team members from the two companies. Disagreements over the technological requirements were never clarified, nor were the disputes among team members regarding roles, responsibilities, and reporting relationships. The project manager believed that these issues "would clear themselves up over time."

During the project planning phase, both the team participants and the sponsors noticed that core priorities had not been established and that key commitments had not been obtained from senior managers. Additionally, the extent of teamwork was minimal because the early personal clashes over roles, style, and status had not been addressed.

What should the project manager have done in this situation? What would constitute a more appropriate approach?

2. What type of project manager is likely to avoid active conflict resolution? Describe some general types of possible conflict "avoiders" that may first be observed during the project initiation phase but will also surface during the remaining project phases.

CHAPTER 6

Stress Management for the Project Manager

What causes stress for you as a project manager?

What do you notice when you answer this question? Maybe an event begins to surface from your memory, something that was upsetting for you. Possibly a feeling begins to emerge, such as anger or anxiety. As you become aware of how you are answering these questions for yourself, consider these "truths" about stress:

- What is stressful for you is not necessarily stressful for someone else.

- Stress is neither good nor bad; all events that are perceived as stressful can have positive components.

The best approach to handling stress is to develop a strong sense of self-knowledge of your personal style, your own sources of stress, and your most adaptive methods for reducing stress.

INHERENT SOURCES OF STRESS IN PROJECT MANAGEMENT

A number of basic project management characteristics create a stressful work environment for the project manager. These include the intrinsic stress of being a leader, the matrix management style of leading, the challenge of solving singular problems, and project ramp-up and ramp-down (see Table 6-1).

Table 6-1. Inherent Stress in Project Management

Source of Stress	Type of Stress Placed on Project Manager	Optimal Stress-Management Approach for Project Manager
Inherent stress of being a leader	Create a "container" for team	Enlist team members to develop a team culture
Matrix management systems	Pressure to build a team quickly and efficiently	Develop skills of influencing others, clear communication, and conflict resolution
Singular problem solving	Challenge of solving unique problems for the first time	Develop the ability to embrace problems and stress on a day-at-a-time basis
Project ramp-up and ramp-down	Demands to energize oneself on intellectual and emotional levels, and an ability to function in an atmosphere noted for a lack of continuity, stability, and predictability	Develop the ability to intellectually and emotionally pace oneself via positive self-talk, diet, and relaxation strategies

Intrinsic Stress of Being a Leader

A project manager faces two types of inherent stressors in the role of leader:

- The pressure to create a culture or "container" in which the team functions

- The tendency for team members to "project" numerous feelings, motives, and attributes on the team leader.

The notion of a leader creating a culture or a container for the team suggests that the leader must expend personal energy and resources to create an atmosphere in which the team will operate successfully. This container for the team does not simply happen; the project leader must strive on a personal level to create the "glue" that holds the team together. This glue consists of team-building efforts that the leader offers to meld the individuals into a unit. Individuals do not coalesce into a team without the leader exerting personal energy to create a bond within the group.

A project manager is applying the glue to bring the team together when he or she:

- Stays late on a Friday afternoon to meet with team members to help them work through a personal disagreement

- Publicly acknowledges the hard work and achievements demonstrated by all team members

- Finds the personal strength to motivate the team after a frustrating period of project delays and setbacks.

The project manager should remember that these efforts require physical, emotional, and intellectual energies. Do not overextend yourself by trying to develop the team culture solely on your own. Enlist team members to display actions and behaviors that help create the glue that bonds the team together.

The second general component of leadership that can prove stressful for the project manager is when team members "project" feelings, attributes, or beliefs on the project manager. In effect, team members are making assumptions that the project manager has certain qualities—either positive or negative.

Project managers enjoy being the recipient of projections that are positive, such as when a team member projects the belief that the team leader is a fair person, possibly because the team leader physically resembles a "fair" person from the team member's past.

Stress, however, occurs for the project manager when team member projections are negative in tone, such as when a team member attributes bad motives to the project leader because the leader reminds him or her of a previous manager with whom he or she had a conflictual relationship.

Examples of problematic projections that team members may direct toward the project manager include:

• Treating him or her as a "parent" (which may have a positive or negative tone)

• Making assumptions about his or her attributes based on gender, race, religion, or age.

If the project manager believes that he or she is the recipient of inaccurate projections from a team member, it is helpful to:

• Schedule time to speak privately with the team member, gently exploring his or her perceptions of you without immediately challenging his or her observations

• Attempt to redefine for them who you are as a person, telling your team about your management style, your beliefs, and how you like to operate.

Matrix Management

Many projects are staffed with individuals who are on loan to the project from other functional areas within the organization. This is the core of matrix management. The project manager may encounter a number of issues and events arising from matrix systems that will be stressful. The biggest challenge for the project manager is influencing people to get the job done while knowing that the working relationship is temporary, lasting only for the duration of the project.

Because the project manager within a matrix system must use influence to obtain results, he or she may experience a feeling of powerlessness when the influencing behavior fails to work. Project managers often report that this feeling of helplessness accounts for a tremendous amount of stress in leading projects.

During situations in which a project manager experiences these feelings of helplessness, stress quickly develops. Internal pressure mounts, and if the experience of helplessness continues unchecked, the project leader loses motivation and initiative.

Some thoughts to keep in mind when trying to manage the risk of stress in matrix systems are:

- Matrix organizations are known for their ability to create a sense of powerlessness, even for the best managers. Do not take the situation personally.

- When "influencing" is not effective, use more subtle forms of personal empowerment, such as making arguments that appeal to the self-interests of the various stakeholders.

Solving Singular Problems

Each project is unique. This quality of singular problem solving represents both the best and the worst of project work. When this characteristic operates in a positive manner, the benefit is that team members get a chance to work on something new and different, unlike anything they have done in the past.

However, solving singular problems can also pose many stressful challenges for the project manager. By definition, the team members have never faced this problem, so there may be no readily available solutions, software, or technology to apply to building the finished product. Everything has to be invented, from the conceptualization and design of the solution to the manufacture of the tools for doing the work.

All these factors place great demands on the project leader. Team members are looking for direction and support and may need guidance on how best to proceed. Emotions of team members may be running high, with people feeling anxious and uncertain, not wanting to take a step and risk making a mistake.

Project managers can handle the stress that comes from solving singular problems by considering the following suggestions:

- Keep motivated by focusing on the positive aspects (e.g., novelty, challenge) of solving a problem for the first time.

- Remember that it is understandable to feel uncomfortable when attempting something new. Avoid self-critical comments such as, "There must be something wrong with me because I can't figure out how to get this solution started."

- Stay in touch with other professionals to determine whether they may be able to suggest problem-solving approaches that may not have been considered.

Project Ramp-Up and Ramp-Down

The periods of project ramp-up and ramp-down can cause pressure and stress for the project manager.

Some individuals react more positively than others to the emotional and physiological ramping up at the start of a project. In fact, some people thrive in these settings, enjoying the rush of energy and the exhilaration that come from starting something new and demanding. These individuals may be referred to as sensation-seeking people who need to have their physical and emotional systems regularly exposed to this type of emotional and physiological activation. During these periods of arousal, sensation-seeking people feel more alive and creative and are often operating in their most positive mood state.

However, not everyone is a sensation-seeking individual, and project managers should not underestimate the demands that ramping up and ramping down can have on the emotional and physiological well-being of their team members as well as themselves. This cycle is demanding and requires that the individual operate in an environment that is intense and constantly changing.

Project managers who repeatedly experience discomfort during this cycle need to take a serious look at whether the role of project manager is the most appropriate one for them to play. Some people, regardless of length of service and best intentions, do not function well as leaders during these demanding periods. For these individuals, taking another role on the team may be a healthier career decision.

Project managers can attempt to take care of their emotional and physiological reactions during project ramp-up by considering these ideas:

- Place avocational pursuits "off to the side" during this period.

- Take each step of the ramp-up process one at a time. Stress and discomfort increase when the project manager creates anticipatory anxiety, which is caused by excessive focus on future events over which one has little current control.

During project ramp-down, the project manager can manage personal stress by remembering that:

- "Endings" involve a sense of loss and frequently a melancholy mood, even when the ending brings great success and achievement. Occasionally, team members may find it difficult to complete the project and finish all the necessary closeout tasks.

- Endings also involve saying good-bye to team members, which can cause natural but unexpected sadness.

- As ramping-down is concluding, it is crucial to take stock of how one is feeling emotionally, intellectually, and physically. Some recharging of the batteries may be necessary, such as a weekend away or time with friends.

Remember, the savvy project manager has a strong self-awareness of how he or she functions during the ramp-up and ramp-down stages and crafts coping strategies to address individual problems that may surface at both ends of the cycle.

PROJECT MANAGER STRESS CAUSED BY DYSFUNCTIONAL ORGANIZATIONS

Organizations operating in dysfunctional ways create stress for the project manager. "Dysfunctional" refers to organizations in which formal or informal processes and culture operate in ways that are not healthy or conducive to a positive work atmosphere. Too frequently, the project manager working in a dysfunctional system becomes a lightning rod for all that is wrong with the organization simply because of the project manager's prominence at the center of the action.

Three key dysfunctional organizational attributes that can cause significant levels of stress for the project manager are: lack of organizational congruence, treatment of people as objects, and dysfunctional leadership at senior management levels.

Lack of Organizational Congruence

Organizations and leaders should demonstrate congruence between spoken or written words and actions. This is "walking the talk." When people or organizations say one thing but do another thing, this lack of congruence heightens the stress level for stakeholders.

A lack of organizational congruence is more than simply a nuisance for team members and project leaders. People who are repeatedly exposed to situations in which a lack of congruence exists frequently display a variety of troublesome symptoms and reactions. For example, when people notice that organizational words and actions do not match, they are often puzzled, saying, in effect, "Am I wrong in my perceptions or is the company wrong?" Self doubt is created, and this self doubt can begin a spiraling process in which the person loses motivation and develops a chronic level of distrust or cynicism.

A situation involving a lack of organizational congruence is a "no-win" situation for the project manager, given that a single project manager is unable to change the culture of an organization. Many project managers experience high levels of stress when faced with this no-win prospect. The best way to avoid too much personal stress in these situations is to seek a middle ground that acknowledges the team members' perceptions about the organizational lack of congruence without getting stuck in too much negativity. A statement that reflects this middle ground is:

"Like you, I also perceive that the company may not be walking the talk on this issue. Let's not spend too much time trying to understand where senior management stands on this issue. Instead, let's focus on what we can do on our level to resolve the contradictions in a way that allows us to go forward and feel as positive and productive as we can about the project."

The tone of this message validates the perceptions of the team member in a manner that is forthright without slipping into company "bashing."

To manage personal stress in situations involving an organizational lack of congruence, the project manager should:

- Be realistic about what can and cannot be done to correct the situation

- Intently focus the team on what can be done on the team level to resolve the discrepancies and keep the project moving forward in a positive manner.

Project managers can get mired in attempting to "right the wrongs" of the organization. Excessive project manager stress occurs when the manager assumes too much personal responsibility for correcting dysfunctional organizational behavior that is beyond his or her control. Do what you can, but take care that you do not ask too much of yourself.

Keep open the option of joining another organization when these forces are too toxic for you to continue working in the current system.

Treatment of People As Objects

Organizations treat people as objects when they adopt policies or methods of dealing with employees in which the individuals are treated as easily replaceable parts. The employees' human qualities are expediently overlooked.

The project manager experiences this objectification as it moves down the organizational hierarchy. Often the project manager is encouraged to continue this objectification toward team members regardless of his or her own personal style.

When the project manager believes that the organization's culture treats people as objects to an extreme, personal stress results. Each project manager must decide whether or not the system is tolerable. Some questions to consider are:

- Can I manage my team in a way that does not treat people as objects and still function successfully in the organization?

- If the answer to the above question is yes, can I do this in a way that does not cause excessive stress for me personally?

Dysfunctional Leadership at Senior Management Levels

Dysfunctional leaders at the senior levels of an organization have a profound effect on creating stressful environments for project managers. Dysfunctional leaders come in many models. Two types that are seldom discussed but can create enormous stress for the project manager are the narcissistic leader and the disengaged leader.

The Narcissistic Leader

Some of the qualities that contribute to successful leadership—a sense of personal self-importance or a preoccupation with success and power—can also be warning signs of the narcissistic leader. The narcissistic leader is so consumed by personal goals and needs that it is nearly impossible for him or her to identify with the needs of others. Occasionally charming, particularly when they want something from others, this type of leader may be known for interpersonal relationships that are exploitative and shallow.

The project manager who must work with a narcissistic leader should do so with great caution. Be careful of this person's charm and interest; it will evaporate when his or her agenda has been achieved. Trust is a one-way street for this person, and the project manager can experience a great deal of disappointment when expecting this leader to recognize the manager's needs.

Project managers can create their own stressful situations when they openly confront this person, going against the person's self-oriented needs. This type of leader does not embrace confrontation, and the project manager who makes direct challenges will feel ostracized and devalued, and will no longer belong in the "inner circle."

There is little that a project manager can do to limit the stress of dealing with a narcissistic leader, since this person's pattern of behavior is character-based and therefore not amenable to change. The best, most realistic strategy for the project manager to use to mitigate this type of stress may be to avoid the person as much as possible or to attempt to create a buffer between themselves and this person. (This buffer could be the head of the organization's Project Management Office—PMO.)

The Disengaged Leader

Stress also flows toward the project manager when senior managers in the organization are disengaged leaders. This is the type of leader whose focus is directed at subjects away from the day-to-day operations of the organization. This person may not be skillful at following through and may not have the necessary systems in place to make the organization productive. The result is that the people who work for this leader are often operating without the necessary systems or resources.

Project managers in an organization with disengaged leaders frequently experience stress related to believing that the leaders have no real interest or understanding about what is taking place on the project level. The project manager has the experience of not being seen or heard by the executive.

In attempting to manage the stress that the disengaged leader can create, the project manager should be aggressive in taking the following actions:

- Look for other sources of support, possibly from other managers or from the PMO.

- Err on the side of action. When working for a disengaged leader, the project manager may be able to manage stress by employing the familiar guideline that says, "It's easier to ask for forgiveness than to ask for permission."

STRESS CAUSED BY THE PROJECT MANAGER'S PERSONAL TRAITS

One's personality can directly contribute to the level of stress that is experienced (see Table 6-2). Four personality traits that contribute to project manager stress are: a perfectionistic-time urgent posture, an over-controlling approach to work, being an overly "feeling" project manager, and unconsciously following certain personal "myths" or beliefs.

Table 6-2. Project Manager Qualities That Can Increase Personal Stress

Source of Stress	Resulting Stress on Project Manager	Adaptive Approach for Project Manager to Use in Reducing Stress
Using maladaptive coping approaches such as: giving up, indulging, denial	Negative habits are reinforced, and stress is never directly addressed or resolved	Stay vigilant for these tendencies, and develop new approaches as needed.
Perfectionistic attitude	Self-imposed pressure (experienced as anxiety, anger, or guilt) to do everything at unrealistic levels of achievement	Realistically consider what is crucial, and lower expectations of oneself/others on tasks not requiring perfect performance.
Tendency to over-control people and tasks	Anxiety, fear that tasks will fail unless "I am intimately involved in all the details"	Look for competency in others, and remember that some things will go wrong but probably can be corrected.
Unregulated sense of time urgency and immediacy	Intensity, anger, anxiety coming from the belief that everything must be done *now*	Pause and ask if this action must be taken now or if it could be done at a later time.
Runaway personal myths (such as the need to play the role of the "hero")	Unrealistic expectations leading to high levels of self-created pressure to pursue actions that may not be realistic	Think through what is motivating your actions, and see if a personal myth is propelling you toward unrealistic or self-defeating actions.

Perfectionism and Time Urgency

The project manager with perfectionistic tendencies under-stands on an intellectual level that perfection is not achievable, but this awareness often is not reflected in his or her behavior. A perfectionistic style combined with a sense of time urgency often has the makings of a Type-A personality (Friedman 1996).

A project manager with perfectionistic qualities and time urgency may hold the following attitudes:

- There is only one acceptable level of performance.

- Anything short of that level of performance will be viewed as a failure.

- Work needs to be done as soon as possible (with little consideration of whether that really matters).

These individuals usually have a large reservoir of internalized anxiety or anger that is a result of the high expectations they place on themselves and others. For this person, a task is not viewed as something to be enjoyed; it is a test of competency and will. Because he or she is so focused on perfection, this person rarely enjoys the journey.

The project manager needs to keep these qualities under control so that they do not cause personal turmoil.

To keep perfectionism and time urgency in perspective, a project manager should consider the following approaches:

- Before a task begins, spend some time listing all expectations—realistic and unrealistic—for your own performance and the result and timing of the project.

- Keep this list on hand throughout the project and refer to it regularly. Determine whether you are allowing yourself to drift into activities that have little impact on project success.

Overcontrol

An ongoing dilemma for a project manager is to define the often nebulous point at which exercising appropriate "control" over a project becomes a matter of "overcontrol."

When not held in check by personal awareness, overcontrol creates stress for the project manager. The project leader is unable to relax, believing that he or she must remain vigilant to control unseen forces or to avoid problems that have yet to occur.

If you believe that overcontrol may be a personal issue for you as a project manager, you can explore that possibility by noting any thoughts that suggest you are trying to take too much responsibility or control for a situation, such as "If I don't personally review all of the technical drawings, something big will be missed and we will fail." After compiling a list of these types of thoughts, ask yourself the following questions:

- What would be the worst consequence if this event occurred?

- What is the risk of that consequence to the overall project?

- How bad is that consequence?

- How could I manage that consequence?

- Could the project and I survive if that consequence actually happened?

The process of delineating fears and worst-case scenarios can have a calming effect on the project manager. Once negative consequences have been explored, a survival plan can be created. This process allows the project manager to let go of some of the emotionally charged aspects of the situation.

The Overly "Feeling" Project Manager

The project manager with a strong tendency toward a feeling style of management is a prime candidate for work-related stress reactions. This person is often described as the "feeling" decision maker on the MBTI (discussed in Chapter 3). As a leader, this individual places a strong emphasis on team morale, interpersonal relationships, and lack of conflict, and takes a personal interest in the welfare and development of team members.

The feeling leader can offer a great deal in the role of project manager. However, this manager is often at personal risk of becoming overly stressed during projects, as a result of his or her strong need to be liked by team members.

The project manager with a feeling leadership style need not abandon this style, but instead must temper and use it cautiously in the workplace.

To avoid the negative consequences of a feeling leadership style in the project setting, this leader should:

- Remember that many team members will view a feeling management style as too personal and too intrusive for the team setting.

- When looking to team members for acceptance, approval, and an emotional connection, consider that you may be attempting to get too many of your emotional and relationship needs satisfied in the workplace. Work to meet those needs in your personal life.

Runaway Personal Myths and Beliefs

All of us have reasons for doing the things we do. Some of these reasons are known to us on a conscious level; other reasons are operating on less conscious levels. Many of the reasons for our doing any task are based on deep, substantive, personal "myths" that we bring with us to the work world.

Personal myths are beliefs that we use to describe ourselves and our motivations in life. Myths are developed in early years and at formative turning points in our lives. An example of a personal myth developed early in life is the belief that says: "I am the smartest kid in my class, and I need to show others that I can solve any problem." Such a personal belief may be grounded initially in fact and then reinforced by teachers, parents, other students, and the world at large.

Personal myths are important because they help motivate us to take action by providing a generalization that we can apply in the workplace. The generalization provides an identity for us—something that tells others, as well as ourselves, who we are. Examples of these identities or personal myths include:

• Hero

• Innovative problem solver

• Brightest person in the group.

Myths serve a positive purpose when they give us a role or purpose on a team. However, if the myth is operating within us on an unconscious level, we may eventually notice that it has taken control of our behavior and has placed us in stressful situations.

Personal myths need to be made conscious. Without having an awareness of what is driving us, we may experience excessive distress, personal pain, and professional problems. How does one become more aware of personal myths? Here is a suggestion.

Imagine yourself as an actor in a film. What role are you playing? How do the screenplay notes and descriptions depict your role and your motives? What actor would be cast as you in the film? The actor you choose gives you a wealth of information about the myths that are driving you. For example, is the actor a famous leading man, previously cast in roles requiring heroic action against overwhelming odds? Is the actress you choose one who is known for roles in which she always does the right thing but is never appreciated by those around her, possibly the earnest, well-meaning victim?

Gaining awareness of our personal myths helps us avoid being managed by them.

ADAPTING TO STRESS: MALADAPTIVE AND ADAPTIVE COPING

Coping methods can be either adaptive or maladaptive. Maladaptive efforts at coping include the following behaviors:

- Giving up, such as stopping an activity in an attempt to achieve some control over the stressor

- Becoming aggressive toward others, such as verbally striking out at people perceived to be causing the stress

- Indulging in the extreme, such as excessive drinking, eating, spending, or playing

- Becoming defensive and overusing denial, intellectualization, or fantasy in an attempt to handle issues.

Most people have employed one or more of these maladaptive coping mechanisms at some time in their lives.

To reduce the tendency to engage in maladaptive coping, the project manager should:

- Develop a personal awareness of possible patterns that indicate when a maladaptive pattern is most likely to surface.

- Remember that some aspects of these maladaptive coping approaches can be positive and helpful in handling stress, as long as they are employed selectively and in moderation. For example, "giving up" may be appropriate when it means stopping work on a troublesome problem one afternoon so that you can go home early, get some sleep, and return refreshed the next day to attack the problem.

Adaptive coping strategies, in contrast, can help the project manager handle and reduce stress (see Table 6-3). Five approaches in particular are useful: using positive psychology, developing resilience, crafting cognitive-behavioral strategies, finding "flow" activities in your life, and using "expressive" tools to release internalized feelings and pressures.

Using Positive Psychology

To use the positive psychology approach to manage stress, a person needs to actively look for the positive aspects of even a very negative or painful situation. In essence, this approach is

---

Table 6-3. Stress Management Tools for the Project Manager

Sociological Tools
- Develop a work-life balance
- Create a personal attachment to your community (however you define it)

Interpersonal Tools
- Spend time with loved ones
- Cultivate multiple, in-depth relationships
- Develop an intimate relationship with a partner-spouse

Emotional Tools
- Use positive self-talk to generate positive expectations
- Use emotional processing tools such as: talking about feelings; personal discussions with a mentor, coach, or counselor; emotional "check-ins" during the day; or free-form journal writing to identify and externalize feelings and emotions

Physical-Somatic Tools
- Healthy diet, exercise
- Relaxation training
- Massage, dance, yoga, stretching

Spiritual Tools
- Meditation
- Awareness of personal values and sources of deep meaning in life
- Active pursuit of activities holding "meaning"

a more sophisticated version of the saying "every cloud has a silver lining."

Researchers have noted that the ability to find the positive aspect of a tragedy or stressful event provides a focus away from the negativity of the situation while also providing the individual with a purpose or mission to embrace going forward.

The following is an example of a project manager applying this approach to deal with project stress.

The project manager was anxious that she had to fly to Europe to complete the work of a team member who had abruptly quit the organization. She was worried that she would not fit in well in this new culture, where she would be called upon to conduct her work in a different language. On the plane ride over the Atlantic, she applied "positive psychology" when she adopted this mindset: "Yes, this can be stressful for me, but it is also an opportunity to work on my language skills and visit my distant relatives."

By crafting a more positive window through which to view the situation, the project manager was able to reduce some of her anxiety and begin to shift to a more positive view of her travels.

It is important to note that positive psychology is not geared toward ignoring the negative or denying the stressful event. These aspects of a project must be acknowledged and addressed. However, positive psychology encourages us to do two things at once: acknowledge the stressful aspect and actively look for the positive aspect of the situation.

Developing Resilience

If you create stress management mechanisms and resources before you need them, you will be more "resilient" when stress hits and you need to respond.

Here's an example of a project manager creating resilience as a stress management method:

Bruce was assigned to lead a product development team in a software company. Fortunately for him, the project was not to begin for three months. Believing that this project was going to be very stressful for him, Bruce decided to work on developing his personal resilience. He started running again, knowing that running helps him sleep well. He called some friends and scheduled regular dinners where he could meet others and share a laugh. Also, he decided to postpone the remodeling effort on his kitchen until next year, wanting to have his remaining weekends free to relax before his big project started.

Using resilience as a coping strategy obviously involves some prior planning, but resilience-creating activities or approaches do not need to be expensive or time-consuming.

Crafting Cognitive-Behavioral Strategies

A cognitive strategy involves monitoring your inner thoughts (those free-flowing, often negative tapes that we play in our thoughts during stressful times) and trying to craft a more neutral or positive internal message.

Negative thoughts, often referred to as "self-talk," flow through our minds without our being consciously aware. An example of this type of negative self-talk could be: *"This project will never work; I've worked with this sponsoring executive before and he can't stand me."*

A more neutral or positive self-talk statement would be: *"While I've never gotten along well with this executive before, it is possible that he might treat me better this time. After all, I've had that big success on the telecom project, and I'm sure he knows about that. I'll try to stay open to the idea that maybe things will be different this time in dealing with him."*

As with positive psychology, cognitive approaches do not suggest that we put our heads in the sand and ignore or deny negative situations. The point is that we must not get stuck in a negative outlook. By creating new, positive cognitions, we give ourselves a more positive outlook to take to the challenging situation.

Finding "Flow" Activities in Your Life

"Flow" activities, according to Csikszentmihalyi (1990), are those special activities in each person's life that give the individual a sense of renewal and happiness. He defines a flow activity as something (e.g., music, sports, reading, a craft, playing with children, walking) where a person loses all sense of time and any feeling of self-consciousness, essentially having the experience of "getting lost" in the activity.

By definition, flow activities do not have to cost a great deal of money or take up large amounts of time. The only requirements for engaging in a flow activity are the ability to identify such an activity in one's life, the basic skill or ability required for successful participation in the activity, and, finally, the willingness to put time aside for the activity.

Using "Expressive" Tools

Talking about personal feelings and issues at work is an example of an expressive tool, which can be very helpful for some project managers. These talks can be with friends, peers, or interested family members. However, depending on the issue at hand, some discussions are best handled through a more formalized relationship with a mentor, an executive "coach," or a personal counselor or therapist.

Some general guidelines to consider when choosing a mentor, coach, or counselor are:

- Choose a mentor when you need someone who has knowledge of your organization or who has been a project manager before and understands what is involved. A mentor can help you navigate some of the political rough spots that you might encounter with the issue in question.

- Choose an executive coach when you want someone who can provide a "neutral" approach to problem solving. A coach will generally help define the problem and then formulate a plan of action that you can implement with his or her support and encouragement.

- Choose a counselor or therapist when you want to address the issue at an emotionally deeper level, examining how certain traits or life events have affected the current problem or are being affected by the current situation.

Personal demands on the project manager are numerous in today's complicated and fast-paced project environment. Stressors facing the project manager come from organizational issues, the inherent complexities of project management, and the project manager's personality traits.

The project manager needs to develop a great deal of personal awareness and understanding in defining his or her sources of stress—what is stressful for one project manager may not be stressful for another project manager.

When creating a personal stress management action plan, the project manager needs to be creative and willing to experiment with different approaches. Unless the project manager is active in identifying the sources of stress and in planning a personalized stress management program, he or she is at risk of being too passive in the face of the stress. Passivity in addressing stress leaves the project manager vulnerable to emotional and intellectual exhaustion arising from a pervading hopelessness that grows from inaction.

A project manager who is fully engaged in a personalized approach to stress management is most likely to remain vital, excited, and content, even in the face of complex demands and challenges.

Discussion Questions

Consider the following situation:

A project manager, operating within a matrix model of organization, encountered significant frustration even before the project got started. This manager discovered that three functional managers were balking at releasing skilled employees to work on the new project. All three functional managers told the project manager that they were understaffed and could not afford to give up good people.

For three weeks, the project leader held meeting after meeting with these functional managers, trying to convince and cajole them into releasing the needed employees. The functional managers' arguments appeared to the project manager as shallow and incomplete. He viewed their actions as being more obstructionistic than professional, and they all appeared to resist any attempt he made to reason with them.

After four weeks, the project manager realized that his anger was increasing, to the point where he was hoping to avoid seeing these functional managers in the hallways. His sleep was interrupted by recurring thoughts of "What am I going to do if I can't get these three people for my team?"

After days of inadequate sleep, he finally appealed to his project sponsor for support—and the three people were assigned to his team. By that time, however, he felt discouraged, fatigued, and unmotivated. And the real work of the project had yet to begin.

1. What should the project manager have done to address these personal feelings before starting work on the project?

2. What would you do if you were in such a situation?

3. In general, what can project managers do to minimize stress while working in a matrix environment?

CHAPTER 7

Critical Incidents: When Traumatic Events Strike the Project Team

A critical incident is a painful or traumatic event that is outside the range of normal day-to-day events and involves some component of loss or harm, such as death or serious injury. The event creates a variety of feelings for the individuals involved, including grief, shock, fear, confusion, or numbness.

Examples of critical incidents include the death of a team member, violence in the workplace, the sudden illness of a team member, the experience of surviving a natural disaster, or being the victim of domestic violence (Herman 1992). Less obvious events, such as the firing of a valued team member or extensive company layoffs, can also be critical incidents.

Critical incidents have an impact on not only the individual team member (the "victim"), but on the team as well. The project manager can take certain actions that will help the individual and the team return to normal levels of productivity. In situations where a critical incident causes extensive disruption to a project team, the project manager may need to implement a project recovery plan—or the PMO may need to bring in a project recovery manager—to save the project.

IMPACT ON THE VICTIM

An individual team member who experiences a critical incident (such as a physical assault) may exhibit a number of reactions and behaviors that will affect his or her work performance. These reactions and behaviors may include:

- *Increased level of fear and anxiety.* The traumatized individual is more vigilant and "on guard," easily agitated by noises, routine fears, or any situation or stimulus that is reminiscent of the traumatic event. Following a trauma, the victim often feels as though he or she is operating "outside" of the body, distant from the normal sense of feeling centered.

- *Somatic problems.* Sleep disturbances, fatigue, changes in appetite, increased risk for illness, and weight gain or weight loss are examples of somatic problems. It is common for some trauma victims to have difficulty falling asleep or staying asleep. Other victims may sleep for 10 to 12 hours every day but still feel fatigued and listless.

- *Temporary cognitive effects.* Decreased concentration skills, a reduction in short-term memory capabilities, confusion, a loss of objectivity, and a diminished capacity to make decisions are examples of cognitive effects following trauma. During the weeks immediately following a traumatic event, victims have difficulty learning new tasks that require significant cognitive focus and attention.

- *Presence of intrusive thoughts.* For many trauma victims, flashback memories of the traumatic event flood their consciousness with little or no warning. What makes these flashbacks so frightening and upsetting is that other sensory experiences accompany the visual memory of the event. Frequently, the victim will notice smells, textures, and other sensory cues that were a part of the original event.

- *Emotional problems.* Depression, emotional numbing, apathy, alienation, and feelings of helplessness and isolation are examples of emotional reactions to trauma. Each trauma victim responds to a situation with different feelings, based in part on his or her personality and history before the event.

- *Issues with substance abuse.* During the tumultuous, emotional periods following a traumatic event, it is not unusual for the victim to seek any form of available relief. Occasionally, this search for relief results in periods of substance abuse as the victim attempts to self-medicate the pain away through excessive use of alcohol or drugs.

HOW CAN THE PROJECT MANAGER HELP?

While the victim needs to take the lead in adopting coping strategies, the project manager can also be helpful by supporting the following activities:

- *Encourage the victim to talk with others.* The project manager can encourage the victim to talk about the experience with appropriate individuals, such as family members and friends.

- *Encourage the victim to continue regular activities.* It also is appropriate for the project manager to encourage the team member to spend casual time with friends and family and stay involved in activities that routinely have been pleasurable in the past. Remember, however, that the trauma victim will probably experience a time-limited decrease of pleasure, regardless of the activity. This is normal, but should not keep the victim from being active.

- *Encourage the use of humor, when appropriate, to get through this period.* Even during periods of crisis, one may be able to find small aspects of the experience that are humorous. These rare moments should be enjoyed, as they become subtle reminders that life may not always look as dark as it looks now.

- *Suggest counseling resources if the problems persist.* It is not the role of the project manager to direct a team member to personal counseling, but such a resource can be very helpful if the victim of the traumatic event feels at some point that he or she is not making progress. Individual counseling or psychotherapy with a professional experienced with trauma can aid the natural recovery process and help the victim move back to normal levels of productivity. The human resources department should have options for such a referral should the team member be looking for professional assistance.

In assisting the victim of trauma, the project manager should remember that the primary goal is to maintain a supportive, understanding, but business-related focus with the affected team member.

- The project manager should avoid the inclination or pressure to become a counselor. He or she should respond with empathy but should also feel comfortable setting some limits on any discussion of the traumatic event.

- When appropriate, consider whether it makes sense to temporarily reassign some of the person's tasks to other team members.

- The trauma victim may ask what other team members know about the details of the traumatic event. The victim may not want to have to tell his or her story repeatedly to all the team members. As team leader, you can pass that request on to the other team members.

- Frequently, trauma symptoms are worse after a week or more has passed following the event; performance may actually decrease over time. Continue to strive toward a posture that is supportive, attentive, and task-focused.

IMPACT ON THE PROJECT TEAM

When a critical incident strikes a member of the project team, other team members will be affected in personal and professional ways. Consequently, the project itself may suffer. The reactions of team members will vary and will often be surprising.

The most common reactions that team members have when a traumatic event happens to a fellow team member include:

- *Emotional reactions.* Team members will display a variety of emotions, including sadness, shock, anxiety, denial, and remorse. Some people will display these feelings immediately, while others will show the feelings after a day or two has passed. Others may display no overt emotion or feeling.

- *Behavior related to workplace duties.* Some team members will talk among themselves for a few hours, with little focus on project work. Other members will ask questions and gather information. Some team members may step forward and volunteer to pick up some of the extra workload.

- *Surfacing of old grievances.* Traumatic events often evoke old issues, angers, emotional injuries, and grievances held by the team members. For example, the death of a team member may prompt a surviving team member to express feelings such as "how the company has always worked people too hard." Often, the old grievances that surface have no direct connection to the current issue. When these feelings surface, the project manager should work to help the team maintain its focus on the current goals of the project.

The project manager may react to a trauma with personal guilt, questioning whether he or she could have done anything to prevent the event. Frequently, the event is clearly out of the manager's control. However, events whose causative factors are less clear, such as an employee who has been working long hours of overtime experiencing a stroke, often cause the project manager to examine his or her own behavior. Specifically, the project manager may wonder if he or she pushed the team member too hard.

When the project manager feels personally "guilty" or "responsible" for the traumatic event of a team member, a personal exercise can help place those feelings in perspective.

Take a piece of paper and divide the page down the middle into two columns. In the left-hand column, list all aspects of the traumatic event over which you had no control. For example, when using this method to address an event where a team member suffered a heart attack when traveling on business, items in the left column could include:

1. The team member's high risk for heart attacks

2. The team member's poor dietary habits

3. Weather conditions, which delayed the team member's travel and increased deadline pressures.

Conversely, entries on the right-hand column should reflect actions over which the project manager does have control, such as:

1. I can continue to push for an increase in staff, therefore reducing team member travel.

2. I can continue to push for "flex time" for the team member as he recovers from the heart attack.

3. I can distribute some of his tasks to co-workers.

This method of listing the "no control" and "have control" aspects of the event is a good way to keep a realistic focus on issues of personal accountability and responsibility. Without this clear focus, it is easy for the project manager to assume undue responsibility for certain types of traumatic events.

CRITICAL INCIDENT STRESS DEBRIEFING

A key recovery strategy for the team that the project manager should consider immediately after the critical incident occurs is to hold a critical incident stress debriefing (CISD). This debriefing is a structured meeting, usually facilitated by a mental health professional skilled in working with trauma reactions, in which employees are presented with the facts of the critical incident and are offered an opportunity to ask questions or share their reactions to it.

The human resources department of most companies can identify a facilitator to lead this type of meeting. The debriefing is not group therapy. However, the CISD helps the co-workers begin to adjust to the loss, planting seeds for the easing of their personal pain, while proactively providing a resource to prevent a significant decrease in team productivity.

Beginning the Debriefing Meeting

The debriefing meeting opens with the project manager telling the team that the debriefer is present to help the team members process their reactions to the traumatic event. The debriefer tells the group that this is a confidential meeting and that verbal participation is voluntary. Generally, a debriefing lasts 90 minutes.

The first step is to go around the room (a small group of three to ten people may be best) and ask each person to tell the group how he or she learned about the critical incident. This step provides a means for facts and details to surface. As team members listen to each other speak, information gaps are filled.

The debriefer does not push people to speak or to bring up strong feelings and emotions. The debriefer asks structured questions (such as, "How did you learn about the incident?") as a method of facilitating the discussion. The debriefer takes cues from the members and does not push beyond what is appropriate.

Letting Members Tell Their Stories

As team members tell their stories, the debriefer periodically augments a member's comments by inserting information about the natural process of going through a trauma. Such a comment may be, "As John is saying, shock and numbness are often big parts of these experiences."

The process continues, with team members occasionally and voluntarily offering favorite memories of the affected person or raising suggestions about how they might help the victim's family. Many of these types of issues have no immediate answers, so some of the CISD process is often spent brainstorming how these personal needs could be addressed at a later time.

Usually, some team members remain silent. Other members may become overly involved in the process, talking too much and taking up too much time. The debriefer will want to be sensitive to this type of situation and will want to help establish some personal boundaries that reflect the purposes and limitations of the debriefing.

Concluding the Debriefing

As the debriefing concludes, the debriefer will summarize the group's general thoughts and reactions. Written materials, often a two-page handout describing common reactions to trauma and what recovery steps can be taken, may be distributed. If the organization has an employee assistance program, the debriefer will provide the phone number, reminding the members that counseling services can be a helpful resource when going through this type of difficult period.

When the debriefing ends, the debriefer, the human resources representative, and the project team leader meet separately to discuss how the meeting went and to discuss any follow-up steps that may be helpful. One of these steps may be to schedule an on-site counselor to be available for voluntary meetings with self-identified employees.

In summary, the goal of the debriefing is to be supportive of the affected team members by providing them with a setting to discuss initial reactions and to receive appropriate information on how to handle the normal processes of recovery and how to return to normal levels of productivity.

WHEN ALL ELSE FAILS: THE PROJECT RECOVERY PLAN

Even in the best of situations, critical incidents can have such a negative effect on the status of the project that the project manager must consider extraordinary measures to save the project from failure. When significant variances exist in the areas of project time, cost, and technical performance, an orchestrated process of immediate salvage should be undertaken. This project rescue effort is known as project recovery.

Variances can easily occur within the context of a project team that has had its efficiency, productivity, and focus disrupted by the turmoil resulting from traumatic events in the workplace. Four indicators in particular suggest that the project is in trouble, and a project recovery plan should be considered:

1. *The project customer is giving signals of being dissatisfied with the product or service or with project status.* These signals can be overt (such as an angry exchange during a project meeting or a critical letter or phone call) or subtle (such as not returning phone calls or minimal participation at project reviews). At the first indication, these overt and subtle signals must be addressed actively. Waiting for the customer to "come around" and regain a positive attitude toward the project is a risky strategy that may result in permanent customer dissatisfaction over the life of the project and in the future.

2. *An excessive amount of project rework is taking place because of poor product quality, team member performance, and technical errors.* Tests fail and peer reviews indicate discrepancies. Project rework is a common by-product for a team that is functioning at temporary levels of diminished capability because of a recently experienced traumatic event.

3. *Levels of unacceptable project variance (in the key areas of project time, cost, and technical performance) have become routine* for this team, possibly because the traumatic event forced everyone to fall behind in their work. Frequently, operating behind schedule causes teams to work in a hurried and rushed manner, thus increasing the probability that the product will have errors that require rework by the team.

This process of rushing to catch up becomes a vicious cycle for the team. "Trying harder" and "working longer hours" do not necessarily mean reducing the key variances. In fact, trying harder often makes things worse and typically increases project costs as overtime is then required.

4. Standard project controls are proving unsuccessful, such as acting on variance analysis or earned value data that forecast potential project difficulties with bringing the unacceptable variances under control. In essence, application of the usual tools and techniques is not getting the project back on track.

In many situations, these four indicators of the need for project recovery are clear to the project manager. However, when dealing with the fallout from a traumatic event on the team, it is easy for the project manager to miss these indicators. Occasionally, this occurs because the project manager sees the symptoms of a problem but is hoping that they correct themselves over time. Clearly, the goal is for the project manager to locate the root cause of the problem and to take action.

Specific Steps to Project Recovery

There are four distinct steps in a project recovery plan.

The first step for the project manager is to *identify actions or alternatives* that will help eliminate the significant variances to project time, cost, and technical performance. Specifically, the project manager should identify ways to minimize damage to the "off-course" project, such as adding or subtracting team members, identifying the need for additional funds or resources, and revising the schedule to expedite a reasonable delivery of the product to the customer.

The second step involves *executing specific actions or alternatives* that may help reduce the project variances. These specific actions could include conducting team-customer meetings to establish a turnaround strategy, holding team-sponsored meetings to discuss possible recovery options, and conducting a tangible, concrete review of the project scope. This process may result in the preparation of a specific project recovery plan, with a schedule of activities to be performed during the recovery efforts and a budget for the recovery initiative.

Once the plan is prepared, the third step is for the project manager to closely *monitor the plan* against the executed actions and alternatives. It is important to review the revised scope of the project frequently, consult with subject matter experts regarding documentation, hold regular status reviews with team members, and then regularly schedule customer meetings, technical reviews, and audits.

Finally, a project recovery process will involve the fourth step of *controlling specifications and alternatives* designed to reduce the unacceptable variances. It is necessary to take actions to minimize the risk of project disaster and ensure that similar project variances do not occur again. The experience and information available from the problems encountered in the current project can be documented in a lessons-learned database or repository and applied proactively to establish risk management responses for future work on the current project and for future projects in the organization.

Assessing Team Effectiveness and Performance

As the project manager begins to craft the four-step recovery strategy following a critical incident, he or she will want to investigate in detail the level of effectiveness of the project team as a unit as well as its individual team members.

Specifically, the project manager should assess the team to determine whether members are using the resources provided to them to meet deadlines and milestones. In addition, performance reports should be reviewed to determine the level of overall team performance.

Another important approach for the project manager is to request feedback from all team members to ascertain how the team is functioning as a unit and how individual team members are functioning when working alone.

The success of the recovery effort is not solely the responsibility of the project manager. Indeed, there are specific actions that the team members must take to assist in the recovery process. It is the duty of the project manager to remind the team members of their responsibilities during recovery.

Team member responsibilities include:

- Informing the project manager immediately as new project problems and risks are uncovered

- Actively supporting the project manager in developing and implementing project recovery strategies

- Regularly updating the project manager on the effectiveness of the recovery strategies, providing frequent status updates regarding project schedule, cost, and deliverables.

IS A PROJECT RECOVERY MANAGER NEEDED?

Even the best project recovery plan is not always successful. In certain situations, the existing project structure (i.e., the project manager and the project team) may be unable to execute the recovery plan. The PMO may then need to identify and appoint a new person to serve as the project recovery manager and reassign the project manager to another initiative.

The recovery manager should be someone who has previous experience with similar projects. He or she should have the skills needed to motivate the team members, work with the stakeholders, make decisions, and hold the team accountable for achieving the project's goals (Rad and Levin 2002).

The primary mission of the project recovery manager is to ensure that project recovery risks are accurately defined, identified, and assessed so that concrete action steps can be taken. The project recovery plan must be clearly described and should be approved and supported by key internal management. Without true meaningful support by management, the plan's chances of success are minimal.

A key element of the recovery plan will be the project recovery manager's review of the assessment results concerning the project and the incorporation of those results into the recovery plan.

Need to Review Progress and Actively Communicate

As the recovery plan is created and implemented, the recovery manager must focus on reviewing progress and assessing future risk. This review and assessment of risk can be accomplished by holding frequent reviews with the project team members. As these reviews take place, the recovery manager is then charged with updating the recovery plan as necessary. Additionally, the recovery manager must keep detailed records and track the financial implications of the action items in the recovery plan.

Another key focus for the recovery manager is to make certain that all lines of communication with senior managers, functional managers, suppliers, and other stakeholders are effective and viable. The recovery manager should be aware of the type of communication that stakeholders require and how often they should receive it.

Consider preparing an analysis of stakeholder information requirements to be certain that the needed information is provided to project stakeholders in a timely manner. Stakeholders should also have access to information in an ad hoc manner between scheduled communications. The recovery manager should update the project's communications management plan and review the effectiveness of the plan frequently. The recovery manager should often ask, "Who else should we be talking with about the needs and status of the recovery effort?" During the stress of a recovery effort, it is easy to overlook a key stakeholder while the team works on day-to-day activities.

Personal Qualities of the Effective Project Recovery Manager

Leading a project recovery effort can be a thankless job, given all the problems that must be corrected and the strong risk of high-visibility failure. This role is not for every project professional.

Leadership Skills

A crucial set of skills for the recovery manager involves the ability to demonstrate "people" leadership skills under trying circumstances. These leadership skills involve the ability to:

- Motivate team members (see Chapter 4) and make difficult decisions

- Hold the work group accountable for achieving goals in a timely manner (the "manager" role discussed in Chapter 2).

The project recovery manager must perform these leadership roles during times of great stress for all involved. Performance of individuals under stress, ironically, is bimodal: Some people improve their performance under stress while others suffer decreased performance.

Traditionally, the most common errors that people demonstrate under stress occur on tasks that:

- Require high levels of concentration and attention to detail

- Involve learning complex material

- Require sophisticated interpersonal skills with team members and other stakeholders.

Interpersonal Skills

The recovery manager should be proficient in applying a wide variety of sophisticated interpersonal skills, including the ability to :

- Resolve conflicts (see Chapter 5)

- Build (or rebuild) the sense of team without critical fault-finding or finger-pointing (see Chapter 2)

Customer Service Skills and Focus

The project recovery manager should also have excellent skills in the area of customer relations. Customer service during situations of project recovery is challenging. The recovery manager must address customer issues forthrightly without becoming defensive.

The project recovery manager should try to understand the needs and concerns of the customer without attempting to defend the previous work of the team. Trying to defend the team at this point creates a "yes, but" interaction between the customer and the team that becomes circular and does not help get the project back on track.

Some project recovery managers enjoy the challenge of the recovery process, but do not spend sufficient time on customer service issues, choosing instead to immerse themselves in the technical content and team details of the project. Typically, it is easier to avoid situations that may be confrontational. This is a natural response, but it can become a serious problem when insufficient attention is paid to the service needs of the customer. The ideal posture for the recovery manager should be to balance time spent working the technical details with time spent addressing customer needs.

When dealing with issues of customer service, the recovery manager should avoid the tendency to over-promise. Some recovery managers may tend to play the hero, swooping in during the crisis and saving the project and the organization's reputation with the customer. The risk in this approach is that the recovery manager may make unreasonable promises to the customer about what can be fixed in the situation.

Any over-promising can come back to haunt the recovery manager, the team, and the organization in not only the current project but also in future business dealings with the customer.

To avoid the risk of over-promising, the recovery manager should:

- Assess and monitor his or her internal need to be viewed as the hero

- Give the customer realistic expectations of what is possible as this becomes known

- Adopt a positive but realistic tone in communications, stressing all that can and will be done for the customer while accurately describing the limits and extent of the recovery possibilities.

Active Communication Skills

The project recovery manager must be assertive in reaching out and communicating with key project stakeholders. These efforts must involve providing regular updates and interacting frequently with management and with customers.

At this point in the project, all stakeholders are aware that things have not been going well, and tensions are high. Stakeholders such as project sponsors and customers do not want any surprises. The best approach to dealing with sponsors and customers is to keep them updated with both the good news and the bad news.

PROJECT FAILURE AND PROJECT CLOSURE

Even with the best efforts, some project recovery efforts following critical incidents will fail and the project should be ended.

The recovery effort—and the project—should be halted when:

- The project has been delayed to the point that the result would be obsolete when completed

- Final costs outweigh the benefits, or no additional funds are available for recovery

- The project is so far out of control that it cannot be managed

- Resources may be better used on other projects.

Although closing down a project is never a pleasant task, it can be handled in an efficient and professional manner.

During the closure process, the project recovery manager should have the following goals:

- Provide accurate and timely information.

- Be direct and clear with all stakeholders.

- Display sensitivity when communicating the reasons for the closure to the various stakeholders.

For many of the stakeholders, the closure will be a personal loss of significant emotional proportion—not to mention the fiscal and reputation losses. Using sensitivity in delivering this bad news can help team members maintain a positive personal, team, and organizational image as they move forward to the next project.

CRITICAL INCIDENT CHECKLIST FOR THE PROJECT MANAGER

Critical incidents in the project world require that the project manager address a number of issues and challenges. The following are key points for a project manager to consider when a critical incident or event strikes the project team:

1. Determine whether a critical incident debriefing should be held for team members.

2. Avoid the temptation during the aftermath of the critical incident to over-promise to team members and stakeholders. You cannot fix everything.

3. Adopt realistic expectations regarding the team members' current ability to perform.

4. Adopt a balanced "yes, but" position with team members, acknowledging that "Yes, we have undergone a crisis and we are all upset about its implications, but we still must find a way to focus on the tasks of the project the best we can."

5. Gradually set boundaries and limits with the team that acknowledge both the loss and the need to stay task focused.

6. Monitor individual work performance, and address possible performance issues by describing the issue and the goal while providing internal and external resources to achieve the desired performance levels.

7. As the aftermath of the critical incident begins to stabilize, determine whether the effect has been sufficiently negative to the progress of the project to warrant developing a project recovery strategy, bringing in a project recovery manager, and reassigning the project manager.

Traumatic events occur to organizations in all industries. These events can seriously affect the emotional life and job performance of individual team members as well as the team as a unit.

When traumatic events strike individual team members, common reactions include emotional distress, poor concentration and motivation, diminished productivity, and impaired interpersonal abilities.

The team as a unit may be helped during this period by having a critical incident stress debriefing led by a skilled and qualified facilitator. The benefit of this meeting is that it provides the team members an opportunity to learn more about the traumatic event, to begin to discuss their reactions to the event, and to ask questions.

In the days and weeks following a traumatic event, the project manager should adopt realistic expectations about team performance, being sensitive to the emotional needs of team members without succumbing to the tendency to become a team member "counselor." Leave the counseling for emotional issues to qualified specialists.

The most appropriate role for the project manager to adopt is that of an attentive and task-focused leader, being supportive of team member reactions while aiding the team in the completion of project work.

Since critical incidents are random events, contingency planning is impossible. Typically, "workarounds" are the only possible strategy. The best the project manager can do is to react proactively to these disturbing events, working with team members and stakeholders to identify both emerging project-related problems and focused resources as quickly as possible.

In situations where the impact of the trauma on the team has been severe, a project recovery plan should be prepared. A project recovery manager should be appointed to assume leadership of the project, and the original project manager should be reassigned to other duties in the organization.

Discussion Questions

A project manager walked into her office on Monday morning and was immediately told by her human resources representative that one of her team members had died over the weekend following a business trip.

This team member, a telecommunications engineer, had suffered a stroke while traveling. This woman had been working long hours for months at a time, frequently volunteering to travel to other states to help fellow team members with difficult projects. Many of the junior team members had looked up to this woman as a mentor and had been trained by her from their first days of employment at the company.

As the team members began entering the building for work that Monday morning, the project manager wondered what she should do.

If you were this project manager:

1. What would be your approach to addressing your team about this issue?

2. What types of reactions and performance issues might you expect from your team members?

CHAPTER 8

Future Issues, Career Management, and Thoughts on People Issues

Future trends related to people issues and leadership have important implications for project managers. Within this context, as a project manager you need to make conscious efforts to improve your performance and actively manage your career. Also, paying attention to the basic qualities of what it means to be a person can enrich your role as a project leader as you and your team members grapple with the many people challenges you face in today's complex world of project management.

FUTURE ISSUES AND CHALLENGES IN PROJECT MANAGEMENT

The profession of project management continues to grow and change at a rapid pace. Professional organizations like the Project Management Institute (PMI®) are experiencing double-digit growth rates, with new chapters being formed on a regular basis.

The growth and sophistication of project management are also evident in a number of other forms. PMI®'s publication, *A Guide to the Project Management Body of Knowledge (PMBOK® Guide)*, has been approved by the American National Standards Institute as an American National Standard. PMI®'s Project Management Professional Certification Program has attained certification from the International Organization for Standardization.

As the profession of project management grows, so do its challenges. The challenges that face project managers are enormous—do it yesterday, do more, finish faster, and use fewer resources. Rapid change seems to be the only constant on projects. As DeCarlo noted (1997), "If you think you're stretched thin now, just wait."

Within this context of rapid growth and change, there are several techniques the project manager can use to improve his or her people skills and thus team performance.

IMPROVING YOUR PERFORMANCE AS A PROJECT MANAGER

The practices of the project manager are at the heart of any successful project. Repeatable, successful projects come from good processes and from project managers who continue to learn and improve their personal practices. O'Neill (1999) noted that people in project management typically spend less than 30 percent of their time on high-priority, value-adding activities. Instead, most of their time is spent coordinating initiatives and working with others—that is, solving people problems. With such a high percentage of time being spent on people issues, it is crucial for every project manager to craft his or her own personal improvement plan.

Crafting a Personal Improvement Plan

In working to create a personal improvement program, the first step is to establish a baseline of your own level of people skills knowledge and competency (Levin 1999).

Assess and document your best and worst performance on projects, with an emphasis on the people skills you used in each case. Note those aspects of your performance that you believed would work well but failed. Also note other situations where you believed that you would not succeed but were in fact successful. These observations will serve as the baseline that will enable you, going forward, to recognize whether your performance is improving or remaining static.

The next step is to define and establish a personal process that you can follow as you perform your project work. The purpose of a process is to describe your intentions, which must meet your needs and help guide your work. Focus on the aspects and areas you can control and influence, as well as on productive activities that add value rather than on circumstances over which you lack control. As DeCarlo (1997) stated, "The next century will put a premium on back to basics . . . challenging us to redirect our energies to focus on those things that are within our power to change. The fact is that we can't change the competitive scene, the course of globalization, or projects that will become increasingly complex."

Establish objective performance criteria for yourself, and compare your own goals with the goals of your manager, your organization, and your customers.

Strive to answer the following questions when creating your personal improvement plan:

- Where does my project fit within the overall strategic plan of the organization?

- Where is my organization headed?

- Why do my projects fail or succeed?

Measure, analyze, and improve your work processes by evaluating the accuracy and effectiveness of your personal plans and processes, making adjustments as necessary. Defining, measuring, and tracking work provide insight into your performance, especially in the area of developing people skills (Humphrey 1995).

However, you should recognize that even with the best intentions, a detailed plan, and a process, some problems will arise. Do not be embarrassed by mistakes you make. Analyze your mistakes and accept responsibility for them. Think proactively and set measurable goals.

Personal improvement can also be viewed from the perspectives of self-mastery and control.

Here are three steps you can take to further your self-mastery in the area of people skills:

- Acquire the training you need to pursue a continuous improvement approach.

- Search for practice opportunities or trial efforts for testing new skills.

- View each project as a way to learn, and share effective practices and lessons learned with others.

Getting By Is Not Good Enough

Frame (1999) believes that one of the two or three most significant issues facing organizations today is competence. In the past, getting by was acceptable; today, getting by is a prescription for failure. Individuals must strive to be superlative.

Cashman (as quoted in LaBarre 1999) offers a similar point on the need to pursue personal growth when he states, "Too many people separate the act of leadership from the leader. They see leadership as something they do, rather than as an expression of who they are." To be more effective in our people skills with others, we must be more effective with ourselves. This means making a commitment to your own personal growth.

IMPROVING THE PERFORMANCE OF TEAM MEMBERS

As you work on improving yourself and your own people skills, you will also be assisting your team members in developing their skills. As you mentor team members (see Chapter 2), you will find yourself offering assistance in helping them grow in many subtle and indirect ways.

To help your team members grow:

• Become a guide.

• Create a team culture of success.

Become a Guide

The project manager must serve as the team members' guide in the project world. Individuals on your team should understand the big picture of the project and should have a clear understanding of how project success is defined. As project manager, it is your job to "guide" your team to this understanding, through the application of your people skills.

To fulfill your role as project guide:

• Meet with team members and foster two-way conversation.

• Talk success and the big picture.

Create a Team Culture of Success

Success must be central to the team culture (Skulmoski and Levin 2001). One method of building such a culture is to structure activities in a way that makes early successes possible. Early successes will help build a winning attitude and set the direction of the project. This effort can help people overcome their fears that this particular project simply cannot be successful. With the habit of success established early in the project, team members will be motivated to continue toward success.

Foster the habit of success by completing a milestone soon so that you can use it to celebrate success with your project team.

For example, reconfigure a deliverable so that a portion of it can be completed early in your project.

CAREER MANAGEMENT FOR THE PROJECT MANAGER

It's your career: What are you doing to manage it?

As a project manager, your career may be just beginning, and you may be enjoying the challenges of developing team leadership skills. Or, you may be in the middle of your career, having had some success but not certain what activities you want to experience over the rest of your career. Or, your career may be fully evolved and you may be curious about what professional activities you could assemble for an active retirement.

Regardless of your current career stage, you must take responsibility for the direction of your career; no one else can do that for you. Even if you are currently working under a benevolent mentor, you may come to work one Monday and discover that your mentor has been terminated or has decided to leave the company. Only you can really be responsible for your future.

The following are six rules for career management and an alternative possibility for a project management career path.

Rule #1: Actively Consider What You Want to Do

The significance of this career rule becomes evident when you listen closely to people who are considering career changes. Many times, professionals say that they never really set a direction for their career. Things just happened.

When you do not take the time to create a system to consider what you really want to do, a situation may develop in which:

- You achieve professional success but never attain personal satisfaction and happiness

- Your current path reaches a dead end, with no alternatives in sight

- Organizational change (merger or downsizing) takes place, and you are caught with no strategy for career survival.

The best way to know what to do with your career is to know who you are. Knowing yourself is frequently the result of placing yourself in situations that provide opportunities for formal or informal self-assessment.

Examples of formal self-assessment experiences include career interest and personal style assessments. Consulting psychologists who are skilled in the interface of personality assessment and career planning often use these instruments to help individuals develop their people skills. Traditionally, these consulting psychologists employ tests that measure:

- Personality and personal style

- Work and career values

- Interest and skill measures.

Depending on the size of your company or organization, you may have a consulting psychologist in the organizational development group or the human resources department. Some project managers value the opportunity to undergo the assessment process with a psychologist who is also employed by the company, believing that this person is intimately aware of career issues within that company. Other project managers, however, prefer to consult privately with an outside psychologist, believing this person will bring a more objective view and perspective to the assessment experience.

Informal, more casual, self-assessment experiences can be equally valuable. These methods are also directed at helping you gain clear information about your personality, your interests, and your values, but do not involve taking "tests."

Informal methods are more self-driven, generally consisting of efforts such as:

- Journal writing, in which you give yourself some quiet, uninterrupted time to write thoughts, feelings, visions, and speculations about who you are, what is important to you, what your shortcomings are, and what your hopes and dreams may be.

- Casual personal "retreats," such as an afternoon or a day off, when you disappear to the local coffee house and ask yourself questions about your career path, unfulfilled career goals, and new directions you could take. These private retreats can be immensely helpful in getting in touch with your internal compass, and require minimal amounts of time or money.

Rule #2: Network, Network, Network!

A professional network is a group of people who have knowledge of you or the trends within your profession. Creating a vibrant and active professional network before you need it is a major ingredient in active career management.

Most professional jobs come from leads generated through professional networks. When you want to make some type of career change or transition in the future, a professional network can be an invaluable resource.

Some examples of people in a professional network include:

- Current and previous co-workers and superiors

- Acquaintances from school, conferences, or professional organizations

- People you know personally or through your community

- People who are known for having their fingers on the pulse of the profession.

There are many tangible ways to develop a professional network. Techniques you can use include:

- Call peers on a periodic basis to find out what is occurring in their professional lives.

- Send selected articles to people who have unique interests.

- Set a goal of meeting three new people at the next professional conference you attend.

- When you receive a promotion or take a new position, inform people in your network of your new activities.

- Create your own personal "board of directors," which is a loose association of people you know who can get together periodically (perhaps over a meal) to advise and guide you through the process of career planning and decision making.

Rule #3: The Higher You Go, the More It Becomes a Matter of Chemistry

As you move to higher and higher levels within an organization, the more that chemistry between people helps further success. You cannot guarantee good chemistry between you and a key executive, but you can work on creating the people skills that give you the capability to experience the chemistry. Good chemistry between people takes place when at least one of the two people has sophisticated people skills.

Closely related to good chemistry is the concept of successfully managing upward toward your functional manager, project sponsor, and other executives. The project manager who can successfully manage upward is able to:

- Understand the needs of his or her manager

- Achieve goals consistent with these needs

- Find appropriate ways to inform the manager about successes and actions in achieving these goals.

For example, if you have a random encounter with an executive or a sponsor, such as in the cafeteria or on the elevator, you should have available a prepared a two-minute summary about your current project. This summary should be in the form of a "sound bite" to discuss rather than simply "small talk." Search for other opportunities to give presentations about your project that will keep internal stakeholders informed.

Rule #4: Keep Your Résumé Current and Active

Any professional in today's fluid work environment should have a résumé that is up to date and polished. Even when you are not currently in the job-search mode, having a current résumé keeps you sharp with regard to recording your accomplishments and prepares you to be interviewed should the ideal job come along unexpectedly.

Make your résumé results-oriented, telling the reader not just what you did (such as "served as project manager for software development") but what you achieved (such as "decreased software turnaround time by an average of 13 percent per project").

A results-oriented résumé:

- Shows that you can set goals and achieve them

- Uses action verbs such as "expanded," "improved," "created," "developed," "reduced," "achieved," and "built"

- Uses numbers to quantify and support your listed accomplishments.

Rule #5: Put Your Personal References in Order

An effort related to creating and maintaining an active, vibrant network is identifying people to serve as your professional references. As with your network, your references should be developed and nurtured well in advance of when you will need them. Do not wait until the interviewer asks you for your list of references; that may be too late.

Once you have a potential job in mind, you need to "qualify" your references. This process involves talking with them about what they expect to say about you regarding the specific job that you are seeking. Tell them what you think the interviewer would want to know about you. Also, tell them something about the specific job and the company that you are pursuing so that they can tailor their comments accordingly.

In qualifying a reference, work to:

- Choose references who will have credibility with the interviewer and whose backgrounds are relevant to the position for which you are applying.

- Inform your reference of the specific accomplishments, traits, and abilities you think the interviewer should hear about. Simply because you remember these accomplishments does not mean that your reference will also remember them.

- Talk with your reference about your specific areas for professional development. You do not want any surprises.

- Make sure that you and your reference are in agreement on the reason you are seeking to leave the organization. You do not want any surprises here either.

Rule #6: Create Your Two-Minute Introduction

As you begin to inform the outside world about your interest in finding a new position, you should be able to tell your story concisely, in about two minutes. A two-minute introduction is the "speech" that you would give to someone who meets you at a conference and asks you to tell them who you are and what you want to do.

Allocate your time wisely when presenting your two-minute introduction. A good rule of thumb is to use about one minute to describe your past and your previous accomplishments and the other minute to describe what you want to do in the future.

The two-minute introduction, tailored to the specific interests and needs of the listener, is designed to quickly and forcefully give the listener the picture of you as an achiever and as someone who is excited and competent to pursue the next venture. You need not specify a particular job when giving a two-minute introduction, but you do need to provide as many details as you can about the setting, the duties, and the role that you want to assume in your next position.

Consider a Portfolio Career

Trends in the workplace have led to the creation of a new way of working—the portfolio career. This type of career can be ideally suited for the project management professional.

A portfolio career is a career in which the individual is involved in a number of professional activities at one time, conducted under the banner of self-employment. In essence, the professional manages a "portfolio" holding the various career activities.

Portfolio careers can be exciting for the professional who wants to be involved in a variety of activities and believes that it is not realistic to expect to find a traditional salaried position in which these varied interests will all be satisfied.

Examples of activities in one person's portfolio career include:

- One day per week of university teaching

- Independent consulting on project management issues

- Coaching project managers on a variety of leadership issues

- Periodic training as a subcontractor for a regional project management consulting firm

- Writing articles occasionally for professional publications.

Portfolio careers are not for everyone, as they have much more variability than salaried positions. In considering a portfolio career, keep in mind that to be suited for such a career, you should:

- Be able to tolerate a lack of predictable structure

- Be comfortable with periods of intense activity followed by periods of minimal activity

- Feel comfortable in an entrepreneurial environment in which you must constantly be pursuing business development efforts.

Some people find it helpful to move gradually from a salaried career to a portfolio career. This gradual move could start with the salaried person teaching a class in the evenings, followed by a shift to part-time salaried work, and then the garnering of the first consulting contract.

THOUGHTS ABOUT PEOPLE

When all is said and done, your biggest challenge as a project manager is dealing successfully with people—people determine your successes and your failures. To work effectively with people, you need to also consider general changes in society.

Tapsott (1998) writes about what to expect with the upcoming generations that come of age in a digital culture. He describes this digitally based culture as one in which people will:

- Exhibit intellectual independence and the need for free expression

- Desire innovation, inclusion, and diversity

- Be motivated by an immediacy in experiences and the acquisition of knowledge.

As a project manager, you should continue to develop the people skills that will enable you to keep up with these evolutionary changes regarding what it means to be a person in this era dominated by technological advancement. The primary people skills that you should continually hone in the digital age are the abilities to:

- Be a persuasive communicator, leading through influence as opposed to directives

- Embrace intellectual and cultural diversity without feeling threatened

- Find ways to comfortably accept the fact that younger team members may know more than you will in terms of current technology and may even be paid more based on their knowledge and skills.

Change is Taking Place, but Do Not Forget the Constants

We all agree that people are changing as a result of rapid developments in the digital world.

However, as a project manager, you should also consider and be aware of the particular aspects of being human that do not change over time. These conditions of being human are often referred to as the existential components of being alive. Although these components do not surface in an obvious form on a day-to-day basis within a project team, they continually affect team member decisions and behavior.

These components will also affect you as the project manager. Your sensitivity to these aspects of being human can help you:

- Have a broader perspective on what makes up a person, including his or her decisions, actions, and sources of motivation

- Find more enjoyment and satisfaction in your work with people, because you can see your efforts and the efforts of others in a much broader context.

Existential Givens of Being a Person

The basic conditions of being human that are often grouped under the heading "existential givens of living" are the conditions of finding meaning in life, how one comes to grips with the condition of isolation, and the unavoidable finitude of life.

Finding Meaning in Life

One of the basic challenges facing any person is creating a personal meaning or purpose in life. The challenge, as we grow and develop, is to define a personal meaning for our individual existence.

Activities that help define one's meaning in life include:

- Self-reflection

- Exposure to different cultures and belief systems

- Guidance from mentors or others in your community.

But what does this need to construct our own personal meaning in life have to do with project management?

In today's world, people are increasingly defining meaning in life as a function of professional and career identity. The concept of "who we are" becomes intricately related to our job description or our profession.

As a project manager, it is important to remember that:

- Each individual strives for his or her own meaning in life, occasionally in ways that may be unacceptable to you.

- You should look closely to find the individual's contribution; the glass really is half full.

From a purely selfish perspective, remember that the more you can understand about someone's approach to finding meaning in life and then give them assignments compatible with that approach, the more successful you will be as a project manager.

Coming to Grips with Isolation

Even the most socially active person experiences, on some level, a sense of isolation and aloneness.

What is this aloneness? It is the fact that no one can ever really know what you are feeling or thinking, regardless of how intent you are in communicating with them. You can try to tell them, but words ultimately cannot bridge this aloneness.

What does this aloneness have to do with project management?

For starters, individuals may choose to work as team members as a means of reducing isolation and aloneness. Sharing a common purpose and developing a common identity can contribute to an individual's interest in working with others on teams. Many find a fundamental comfort in having an identity that reaches beyond their identity as individuals.

As a project manager, do not underestimate the power that the team has in reducing the experience of individual isolation. Treat the formation of "the team" and the ongoing treatment of the team with honor, respect, and care. For both you and your team members, the team is more than simply a vehicle for accomplishing a task. Treat the need for this connectedness with respect and care.

Remember that the team is an evolving entity through which:

- Individuals can feel part of something greater than themselves

- People are offered a chance to work together toward a common purpose, decreasing alienation and isolation.

Managing Beginnings and Endings

Projects and people have one basic quality in common: both have a beginning and an ending.

Many of us manage our anxiety about our ultimate demise by becoming very active in our work. This is not necessarily bad. In essence, work becomes a medium through which we can create testimonials to our time on earth, establishing concrete representations of our labors and our achievements that will remain after we are gone.

Work can be an effective means to come to grips with the fact that our life span is limited; this in part explains why people will work outrageous hours or put up with nasty bosses or co-workers. We want to leave this life with some marks of achievement, something that will outlast us.

Because we want to leave testimonials to our lives via our work, we work hard, sometimes too hard. As a project manager, it is important for you to realize that each of your team members wants to leave his or her testimonial through their work; this need surfaces on some level over the course of each project.

Help team members enjoy the experience of leaving a personal legacy or testimonial through their work on each project by:

• Helping them have successes on each project

• Helping them understand that their work makes a difference.

PARTING THOUGHTS

The role of project manager is special. It goes beyond the specifics of shepherding a project to completion. You influence the lives of people who are looking to you for guidance, and you affect the vibrancy, level of excellence, and future capabilities of your company or organization.

Try using the tools and approaches presented in this book. Above all, remember that solving people issues requires that you use your people skills as an artist would use his or her skills: practice, experiment, integrate, and trust your intuition. Project management can be a highly rewarding position on both the professional and personal levels.

References

Buber M. 1970. *I and thou*. New York: Charles Scribner's Sons.

Bugental, J. 1990. *Intimate journeys*. San Francisco: Jossey-Bass.

Cleland, D.I. 1999. *Project management strategic design and implementation*, 3rd. ed. New York: McGraw-Hill.

Csikzentmihalyi. M. 1990. *Flow: The psychology of optimal experience*. New York: Harper Collins Publishers.

DeCarlo, F.D. 1997. *It's gonna be a jungle out there managing projects in unfriendly cultures: How to survive and thrive in the next century*. Proceedings of the 28th Annual Project Management Institute, Seminars & Symposium, Chicago.

Flannes, S. 1998. *Choosing the team that really works: How an understanding of personal style helps your team succeed*. Proceedings of the 29th Annual Project Management Institute, Seminars & Symposium, Long Beach, CA.

Flannes, S., and D. Buell. 1999. *Coaching skills for the senior human resource professional*. Unpublished paper and seminar presented to the Northern California Human Resources Association, August 12, 1999, San Francisco.

Frame, J.D. 1994. *The new project management: Tools for an age of rapid change, corporate reengineering, and other business realities*. San Francisco: Jossey-Bass Publishers.

Frame, J.D. 1999. *Project management competence: Building key skills for individuals, teams, and organizations*. San Francisco: Jossey-Bass Publishers.

Friedman, M. 1996. *Type A behavior: Its diagnosis and treatment.* New York: Plenum Press.

Hammer, A.L. 1996. *MBTI applications: A decade of research on the Myers-Briggs Type Indicator.* Palo Alto, CA: Consulting Psychologists Press.

Harvey, J. 1988. The Abilene paradox: The management of agreement. *Organization Dynamics* 17(1):16.

Haywood, M. 1998. *Managing virtual teams: Practical techniques for high-technology project managers.* Boston: Artech House.

Herman, J.L. 1992. *Trauma and recovery: The aftermath of violence, from domestic violence to political terror.* New York: Basic Books.

Humphrey, W. S. 1995. *A discipline for software engineering.* Reading, MA: Addison-Wesley.

Jung, C. G. 1971. *Psychological types, collected works,* vol. 6. R. Hull, trans. Princeton, NJ: Princeton University Press.

Kerzner, H. 1998. *In search of excellence in project management: Successful practices in high performance organizations.* New York: Van Nostrand Reinhold.

Kirby, L. K., N. J. Barger, I. Briggs-Myers, and R. R. Pearman. 1998. Uses of type in organizations. *MBTI Manual.* M. H. McCaulley, N. L. Quenk, and A. L. Hammer, ed. Palo Alto, CA: Consulting Psychologists Press.

LaBarre, P. 1999. How to be a real leader. *Fast Company* 24, May 1999.

Levin, G. 1999. *Aspiring to peak performance: A personal improvement model for project management professionals.* Proceedings of the 30th Annual Project Management Institute, Seminars & Symposium, Philadelphia.

Lewin, K. 1948. *Resolving social conflicts and field theory in social science*. Washington, D.C.:American Psychological Association.

Maslow, A. 1970. *Motivation and personality*. New York: Harper & Row.

Meredith, J. R., and S. J. Mantel, Jr. 2003. *Project management: A managerial approach*, 5th ed. New York: John Wiley & Sons.

Noer, D. 1993. *Healing the wounds: Overcoming the trauma of lay-offs and revitalizing downsized organizations*. San Francisco: Jossey-Bass Publishers.

O'Neil, J. 1999. Short-staffed? Maximize scarce resources with knowledge resource planning. *PM Network* 13:37.

Packard, T. 1995. TQM and organizational change and development. *Total quality management in the social services: Theory and practice*. B. Gummer and P. McCallion, ed. Albany, NY: Rockefeller College Press.

Peters, T. 2004. Nix the spreadsheet. *PM Network*. January 2004. Newton Square, PA: Project Management Institute.

Rad, P., and G. Levin. 2002. *The advanced project management office: A comprehensive look at function and implementation*. Boca Raton, FL: St. Lucie Press.

Rad, P., and G. Levin. 2003. *Achieving project management success using virtual teams*. Boca Raton, FL: J.Ross Publishing.

Schein, E. 1990. *Career anchors: Discovering your real values*. San Francisco: Jossey-Bass/Pfeiffer.

Skulmoski, G., and G. Levin. 2001. Creating the environment for successful projects: 5 key ingredients for project managers and project participants. *ESI Horizons* 2(9), January 2001.

Tapsott, D. 1998. *Growing up digital: The rise of the net generation.* New York: McGraw-Hill.

Thamhain, H. J., and D. L. Wilemon. 1975. Conflict management in project life cycles. *Sloan Management Review.* Summer 1975, 31–50.

Thomas, K. W., and R. H. Kilmann. 1974. *Thomas-Kilmann conflict mode instrument.* Palo Alto, CA: Consulting Psychologists Press.

Verma, V. K. 1997. *Managing the project team.* Newtown Square, PA: Project Management Institute.

Index

Breinigsville, PA USA
03 March 2011
256921BV00004B/1/P